DESIGNING USER INTERFACES FOR SOFTWARE

JOSEPH S. DUMAS

DESIGNING
USER INTERFACES
FOR SOFTWARE

Y 1 0 2

DESIGNING
USER INTERFACES
FOR SOFTWARE

Joseph S. Dumas

American Institutes for Research

Prentice Hall, Englewood Cliffs, New Jersey 07632

Library of Congress Cataloging-in-Publication Data

DUMAS, JOSEPH S. (date)
Designing user interfaces for software.

Bibliography: p.
Includes index.
1. Computer software.   2. Computer interfaces.
I. Title.
QA76.754.D86 1988   005.1   87-7178
ISBN 0-13-201971-X

Editorial/production supervision
and interior design: Elaine Lynch/Gertrude Szyferblatt
Cover design: Wanda Lubelska Design
Manufacturing buyer: Paula Benevento

ISBN 0-13-201971-X 025

Prentice-Hall International (UK) Limited, *London*
Prentice-Hall of Australia Pty. Limited, *Sydney*
Prentice-Hall Canada Inc., *Toronto*
Prentice-Hall Hispanoamericana, S.A., *Mexico*
Prentice-Hall of India Private Limited, *New Delhi*
Prentice-Hall of Japan, Inc., *Tokyo*
Simon & Schuster Asia Pte. Ltd., *Singapore*
Editora Prentice-Hall do Brasil, Ltda., *Rio de Janeiro*

CONTENTS

PREFACE

A computer program I recently used displayed a message indicating a "MISCELLANEOUS PERMANENT ERROR." I clearly had done something I shouldn't have. What I did, however, is still a mystery to me. Whatever I did cannot be described in a specific way. It's "miscellaneous," and its effect is somehow "permanent." Since I gave up trying to use the program, the error certainly was permanent.

This error message made me angry at the designer who created it because it does not tell me what I did wrong or how to correct it. On the other hand, there are many new computer users whose reaction would be to doubt their own ability to communicate with computer programs. It may also confirm their suspicions that computer technology is something they cannot cope with. Unfortunately, their suspicions may be correct, not because of the technology itself, but because of the way the interfaces to many software programs are designed.

The theme of this book is that computer software must be designed from the user's point of view and tested with potential users to ensure that they can readily make it work. Designers of software and its users communicate with each other through the interface to the software. Designers who realize this have taken the first step toward creating better products. The next step is to follow the rules and guidelines described in this book.

What is an interface? *Webster's Seventh New Collegiate Dictionary* defines an interface as "the place at which independent systems meet and act upon or communicate with each other." My objective in writing this book is to help you to improve the design of a particularly important interface, namely, the place where human beings and computer programs meet to communicate with each other. The components of this user-software interface that I am concerned with are the words and symbols that people see and read on the computer screen; the content and layout of displays; the procedures used to enter, store, and display information; and the organizational structure of the interface as a whole. While the term "user-software interface" is an awkward string of nouns, I hope that you will forgive me for using it since I know of no other term that clearly describes the place where people and software meet to communicate.

- WORDS
- GRAPHICS
- LAYOUT
- PROCEDURES
- STRUCTURE

Figure 1 What Is the User—Software Interface?

I will not use the term "user-friendly" to describe an interface that is designed according to the rules I describe in this book. This term has been used to promote so many poorly designed programs that it has lost its meaning. For example, the designer of the program with the error message I described earlier claimed that the software was "user-friendly." Software manufacturers who use this term in their promotional literature now sound more like used-car salesmen than competent software vendors. This is unfortunate because there are no other terms that describe a software program that allows its users to communicate with it as easily as with a friend. Consequently, I will use adjectives such as "good," "better," and "effective" to describe user interfaces that are designed according to the principles and guidelines in this book, and I will explain what these adjectives mean when I use them.

There are three audiences for this book:

- Professionals who create software
- Project managers who guide its development
- Students who are learning about software development

The first audience for this book consists of those professionals who design, implement, and evaluate the user interface to software programs: software engineers, systems analysts, programmers, testers, and evaluators. Consequently, I have assumed that they are familiar with basic concepts and terms, such as "cursor," "mouse," and "window," that describe the components of a typical interface.

This book is intended, however, for a much wider audience than just those people who are directly involved with interface design. There is more to creating effective user interfaces than just knowing the design rules. Developing computer programs that are not trivially small is a group process and, if the group effort is to be effective, everyone must be following the same rules. For this to happen, companies that develop software must establish a set of policies and procedures for creating and disseminating the rules and must provide some incentive for people to follow them. Thus, the management of these developers is critically important to its improvement. Consequently, there is a second audience for this book; the project managers and system designers who have overall responsibility for the development of software products.

The final, but by no means least important, audience is students of computer, behavioral, or management science who expect to become involved in the development or evaluation of software. Until recently, the principles of user interface design have not been part of university programs. Fortunately that trend is being reversed. Effective design practices are being taught in courses in several different departments. If you are a student in one of these courses, this book will provide you with a basic understanding of the principles of user interface design and how to implement them.

The material in this book comes from three major sources: my experience working with software designers to help them create and evaluate the user interfaces to their products, my knowledge of the research literature of human-computer interaction, and my experience and training as a cognitive psychologist. Over the last few years, I have spent thousands of hours working with software engineers and programmers to help them (1) design and improve their user interfaces and (2) test the usability of their products. During this time, I have read and contributed to the human factors literature and talked extensively with my professional colleagues. I have been frustrated in my work with designers and their managers by the lack of a single source that describes and interprets the accumulated knowledge about human-computer interaction that professionals working in this area discuss with each other. I have been repeatedly asked by clients for a reference that will tell them how their organization can improve the user interface to all of their future products. I have tried to create that reference in a practical form, that is, one that you can understand and implement.

Until a few years ago, the literature primarily contained descriptions of the problems with existing interfaces and a few broad guidelines for designers. More recently, the literature has exploded. There are now many research studies that provide empirical confirmation that good human factors practices do indeed make a difference in the productivity and satisfaction of users. Where they are relevant, I have referred to these studies throughout the book. However, I do not claim that all of the rules I recommend to you in this book are built on a foundation of research studies. If I restricted myself to such rules, this would be a much shorter book. Unfortunately, the literature does not describe a coherent science of human-computer interaction or an accepted theory of how people and computers interact. As a consequence, practitioners such as myself have had no comprehensive theoretical basis for emphasizing some practices while ignoring others. I have, however, tried to give my proposed rules and guidelines some clear rationale by relating them to a set of general principles of interface design that I describe in Chapter 4. Those principles and the guidelines that follow are not the last word in user interface design. They are, in fact, just a starting point, a foundation on which to build. As you will see, we are only beginning to understand how people and computers interact.

This book's eight chapters are divided into an introductory chapter and two major sections. Each chapter begins with an Overview that provides a road map to the chapter. Section I, which contains chapters two and three, describes how to manage the development of the user-software interface and how to create a user-interface handbook for your project team or organization. If you are a project manager or system designer who has overall responsibility for a software product, you will find this section particularly useful because it describes, in detail, how you can establish a process to manage the user interface for all of your future products. If you are a student, a software engineer, or a programmer who works on a software development team, you will be interested in this section to see what it will take to get all of the members of your team and all of the other teams in your organization to follow the same rules.

Section II, which contains the last five chapters, describes the principles of interface design and the guidelines that provide the foundation on which you can build more effective user interfaces. If you are a project manager, you will be interested in this section to see what guidelines your staff should follow to create products that are easier for users to learn and use. If you are a software engineer, programmer, or student, you will be primarily interested in this section because it describes each of the guidelines in detail and illustrates how to implement them by showing you examples of both poor design practices that you should avoid and good practices that you should follow. Throughout this section I indicate how you can tailor these practices for your project team or organization. Finally, the appendix contains a list of all of the guidelines in the book cross-referenced by chapter and page number.

It is always difficult to credit everyone who contributes to a book. Of the many colleagues at the American Institutes for Research who provided encouragement and support in the preparation of this book, I would like to especially mention:

- Mike Sadofsky, who provided encouragement throughout and who made valuable comments on the early drafts
- Ginny Redish, who, in our work together, helped clarify many of my ideas and who taught me how to communicate those ideas more effectively
- Amy Smith and Beth Parish, who helped create the graphic illustrations

Gary Klein provided support when I needed it most and kept me from wavering from my primary objectives.

Finally, my wife, Martie, kept my spirits up and scrupulously edited the drafts of the manuscript. She taught me that every sentence does not need two "thats," though even she would agree this one does.

Chapter 1

Taking
the User's
Point of View

OVERVIEW

As a software designer or manager of a software development team, you and most of the people you know are comfortable with computer technology. There are, however, many new computer users who question whether computers will ever help them at work or at home because of their first experiences trying to use this new technology. Software professionals tend to see a product from the point of view of the structure of its software. Users tend to see the product as a tool to help them get some task done. "Designing for the user" requires that you see the product from the point of people with a particular set of computer and technical skills, trying to get some job done in a particular environment.

The current gap between the skills of designers and those of users has, to a substantial degree, been caused by the poor interfaces and documentation that have been provided with software in the past. Sections I and II of this book provide guidance on how to design effective user interfaces and how to set up a process to ensure that effective user interface practices are followed consistently. Section I describes a series of steps you can follow to set up a process which can ensure that you and your organization put the proper emphasis on the interface during design and apply that emphasis to all of your products. Section II describes general principles of interface design and offers specific guidelines and practices that will make your design conform to the principles.

There is a widening gap between the capabilities of computer-based systems and the ability of people to use those capabilities. The computer hardware and software currently available provide us with the potential to complete work more quickly and with higher quality than ever before. Computers, however, are still a new tool to many people and their ability to make use of them is limited by, among other things, the clumsy, inconsistent, and frustrating software interfaces they encounter. The goal of this chapter is to show you that as a software designer or manager, you are on one side of this gap — the side with the sophisticated, experienced users. The first step to creating better software interfaces is to begin to see the products that you are developing from the end user's point of view.

THE TECHNOLOGY AND ATTITUDE GAP

You and most of the people you know are comfortable with computer technology. If you are like many of the people that I know who create software, you are totally immersed in computer technology at work and at home and you are excited by opportunities to explore its limits and new products. You may also share an attitude with many of your colleagues that many people on the other side of this gap who are not excited about this new technology are so rigid that they refuse to see the obvious. I believe, however, that many of the new computer users who question whether computers will ever help them at work or at home do so because of their first experiences trying to use this new technology. The examples of poor user interfaces that I have spread throughout this book should convince you that these people have a legitimate gripe that computer software has not been created for them because its designers have not taken the time to understand their point of view. Some specific examples may help you to see what I mean.

EXAMPLES OF THE GAP

As an employee of a consulting firm, I have had the opportunity to work with people on both sides of this gap. I have worked on projects with designers and managers of software products to help them manage their software interface design process more effectively and to produce better interfaces. At the same time, I have worked with the management of organizations, big and small, that are buying these products and trying to use them to make their workers and themselves more productive. In serving these two very different types of clients, I have observed two gaps: (1) the gap between the capabilities of the products that manufacturers are producing and the ability of office workers to make these products work for them and (2) the gap between the attitudes of the designers of the products and those of their users.

Recently, my company had the opportunity to work with an organization of over five hundred employees to help them more effectively use the microcomputers they had recently purchased. Among other activities, we interviewed all the people in the organization who had access to a microcomputer. We asked them what their training needs were, but we were really interested in what they were using their microcomputers for, if anything, and why they were not using them to their full capabilities if, as management suspected, they were not. We found that a few individuals were using their machines in their everyday work. Almost all of these people had personal computers at home. The rest of their colleagues were either not using their computers or were using them only for word processing. When we asked these people what they felt they needed to know to use their machines more effectively, they listed the following:

- *How do I get the microcomputer to work?* Many of these people could not even get started. They had never formatted or configured or copied a diskette before, and all of these operations had to be done before they could use any of the software.
- *How do I find the information I need to get my work done?* The four-volume set of manuals for the computer was written in the same style as manuals written for programmers and computer operators. The end users frequently could not find the information they needed because the manuals did not include headings that refer to the tasks that users want to learn about, such as "How to get started." Furthermore, when they did find the information, they couldn't understand it.
- *How can I understand how the software operates?* Many people who were helped to get started by their more computer-literate colleagues were stumped by not knowing what they could do when they finally did get the machine to say:

A>

Users who were savvy enough to type a question mark received an alphabetical list of commands. If they typed HELP and a command name, such as COPY, they received a message that gave them a technically precise but incomprehensible definition of the format of the command. Those who explored further were frustrated and angered at the clumsiness of the interaction with their computer. For many people this experience confirmed their belief that computer software is not designed for inexperienced people.

- *How can I use the machine to help me do my work?* From a consultant's point of view, this is the most interesting question. Answering it requires raising the level of awareness of these people about how technology can work for them. Most people, however, in this organization never got to this question because the barriers that the technology placed before them confirmed their attitude that struggling with this new tool would not make them more productive.

At the same time that these interviews were being conducted, I also had the opportunity to work with several software developers on what they classified as "human factors" problems, problems that are probably similar to those you have faced. These developers are trying to harness the new technology that is available to them. For the most part, however, they do not realize how little experience most people have with the old technology.

One of these developers asked me to do a "human factors" assessment of one of their products. The objective of this product was to allow users to quickly create graphics for briefings (the type of graphics that are printed on transparent plastic and shown on an overhead projector). The first task that the product asked the user to do was to enter the name of the style of graphic that they wished to create, such as a word chart, a pie chart, or a bar chart. The designers, however, saw this first step as a way to retrieve data from one of many files that contained information about each style of chart. They had given these files names that looked like arbitrary combinations of characters. For example, "H5.PVF" was the name of the bar chart file. Actually, the "H5" refers to the style of chart. The "PVF" is a filename extension that the designers had given to all of the files that contained information about the chart styles. Throughout the course of development they referred to these files as "prompting visual files," hence the "PVF."

The designers of this product made a decision, by default, that caused users frustration and anger. They forced users to enter the filenames that they, the designers, had created rather than allowing users to enter meaningful names and then translating them, in the software, to the filenames. Instead of allowing users to enter "bar chart" or having users pick from a list of names, they made users enter "H5.PVF." Of course, they realized that some users would not remember all of these names, so they put a list of them in the user's manual. This was their solution to the problem.

The users' problems did not end, however, with remembering the names of the charts. When they made an error typing the name, their confusion was intensified. For example, if users forgot to put the "PVF" extension on the name and just typed "H5," they received the following message:

```
ERROR TRYING TO OPEN H5 FILE   ERROR NUMBER 51
```

This message makes no sense to most users. What does opening a file have to do with the name of the style of chart to be created? What is "error number 51"? The user simply does not know what to do at this point. This error message is actually generated by a computer system utility when the filename extension is not correct. The designers compounded their earlier decision to make the user enter filenames by allowing this error message to be passed directly to the user without translating it into terms that explain what the user did wrong and what to do about it.

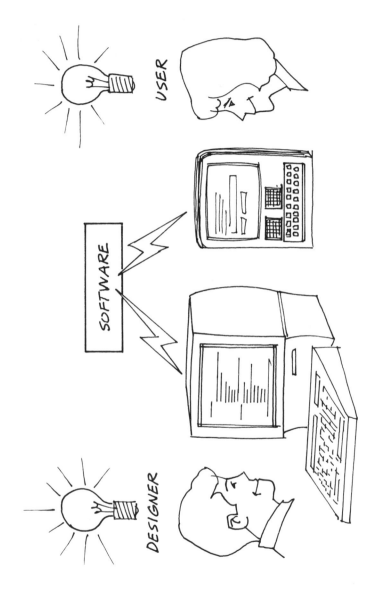

Figure 1-1 The Interface: A place to communicate.

There were many other problems with this product. But the point here is that the designers simply did not consider the user's point of view when they were designing the interface, even though they said that they wanted to create a "user-friendly" product. The designers are very clever people whose product is not successful because they designed it without considering the user's point of view and because of their attitude about the capabilities of their users. The designers are bright people trying to harness the tremendous capabilities that computer technology now provides. They see themselves in a race with their equally bright colleagues working in other companies, perhaps like yours, to produce a product that will give them a bigger segment of the market. To do this they must explore the limits of what is new to them. It is not in their nature to do otherwise.

I believe that software professionals project their own experiences and attitudes onto their users. Designers often have a wide range of experience with other systems, can easily get help from their peers, and have the desire to explore new tools. However, the text editors and command languages they learn to use often have clumsy and inconsistent terminology and procedures. The difficulty of using these tools is compounded by the poorly designed and written documentation that accompanies them. Furthermore, software designers are often expected to learn these tools without formal training. Despite these barriers, designers forge ahead to master new tools. They treat the barriers as challenges to be overcome. They experiment and explore until they have learned what they need to do a better job.

It is difficult for designers who take this active approach to realize that most people still do not use computers on a regular basis. Because most users do not understand the basics of computer systems, they are afraid to explore the capabilities of new products. They are trying to get a job done and they learn only enough to accomplish it. When the interface makes using an application difficult, users may quickly give up in frustration and never try again.

BETTER INTERFACES CAN NARROW THE GAP

This gap between the capabilities of computers and the people who are trying to use them will not be easily closed. I believe, however, that the current gap has, to a substantial degree, been caused by the poor interfaces and documentation that have been provided with software. Throughout this book I will show you many examples of poor interface design practices that make users frustrated and angry. Improving these practices can help close the gap, but the improvement must begin with a change in point of view. It is important that you understand the level of computer literacy of your users and realize that it is your job to communicate with these people through the interface to your software. Looking at the product you are developing from the user's point of view is the first and most important step in improving its interface.

This book focuses on the user interface to software. The interface, however, is only one component, although a very important one, of a successful product. The usability of a software product depends on a number of components in addition to the interface, such as documentation, training, and most importantly the functionality that the product provides. It must help the user get a job done by making it easier or faster or less costly. It may also provide additional capabilities to users and improve the quality of their work. If it does not provide functions that are at least comparable to its competitors, an effective interface is not likely to make it a success. But if the functions are competitive, the quality of the user interface can determine a product's success or failure.

My intention in writing this book is to create a practical guide to producing better user-software interfaces and, therefore, better products. The emphasis is on the word "practical." I do not believe that any one source in the voluminous literature now available contains the information you will need to improve your software. The literature contains an abundance of good advice and an overwhelming number of lists of guidelines. Section II of this book contains the most important of these guidelines. I have carefully chosen those that, in my experience, have provided the most basic understanding of interface design. Rather than just listing them, I have described them in detail and have illustrated them with examples to show you how to interpret them. If you need a complete list of all of the guidelines currently in print, see Smith and Mosier (1986).

But the guidelines in this or any other book will not solve all of your design problems. Guidelines are simply a convenient way to communicate the accumulated experience that human factors and other related professionals have obtained from their work and their research. By their nature, guidelines frequently do not speak directly to new technologies or to new ways to use old technologies. You will have to extrapolate and tailor the guidelines to your needs and, if you work with a team of people, set up a process to manage implementation of the guidelines. What is needed, in addition to guidelines and rules, is a set of organizational procedures and a management structure to guide the interface development process.

Section I describes the steps that you and your organization can take to set up a process to manage your interface development from the user's point of view. As I will show in the next chapter, if you do not follow these or some equivalent steps, you will find it difficult to produce better interfaces consistently. The user interface to software requires special attention throughout the development process by people with special attitudes, skills, and experience. It takes commitment and resources to make the process work. I hope that by describing the steps you will need to follow to manage your interface development process, the gap between the capabilities of the software you will be producing and the abilities of your users will be narrowed.

SECTION I

MANAGING
THE DEVELOPMENT
OF THE SOFTWARE
INTERFACE

Chapter 2

Establishing
the Management
Process

OVERVIEW

Implementing a set of user-interface guidelines, such as those described in Section II of this book, is necessary but not sufficient to allow your organization to improve its user interfaces. You must also establish a process to manage user-interface development if your organization is to produce better products consistently.

The six major steps suggested to establish an interface development management process are:

1. Obtain the support of management.
2. Set goals that your organization can achieve.
3. Create a user-interface handbook that describes the guidelines and rules your staff should follow.
4. Emphasize the guidelines and rules throughout the software development process.
5. Conduct usability tests of the interface.
6. Keep your handbook up-to-date.

Over the last few years I have observed a change in the attitudes of designers and project managers toward the user interface. Until recently most developers had to be convinced that their interfaces needed substantial improvement to be merely adequate from the user's point of view. Many of these designers simply did not believe that the user interface was important and managers were skeptical that a better interface would sell more products. More recently, designers and managers have come to believe that improving the user interface is a goal worth working toward. They also frequently admit, however, that they do not know how to achieve that goal. Many managers do not know what steps to take to move their organizations toward creating more usable products. They frequently feel that hiring the best software professionals and demanding modern software development techniques is the answer. Still, the user interface to their products lags behind the overall quality of the software. Why?

If you, as a product or project manager have been trying to change the way your team or organization creates its user interfaces, you know that an effective software interface does not happen by itself. Furthermore, you cannot guarantee that good interfaces will be produced just because you hire well-trained and experienced software engineers and implement structured software development techniques. Creating a good interface requires a special organizational effort that is comparable to that needed to improve the

other components of good software.   It takes the commitment of
management, a knowledgeable staff of people who understand the
principles of user-interface design, a set of good tools, including
user-interface guidelines, and the establishment of policies and procedures to meld these components together into a process that controls interface development.

The theme of this chapter is that implementing a set of user-
interface guidelines, such as those described in Section II, is necessary but not sufficient to allow your organization to improve its user
interface.   You must also establish a process to manage user-interface development if your organization is to consistently produce better products.

In this chapter, I will describe the six major steps that I believe
must be followed to establish an interface development management
process:

1. Obtain the support of management.
2. Set goals that your organization can achieve.
3. Create a user-interface handbook that describes the guidelines
    and rules your staff should follow.
4. Emphasize the guidelines and rules throughout the software
    development process.
5. Conduct usability tests of the interface.
6. Keep your handbook up-to-date.

If you follow these steps, you will be able to establish the condi-
tions necessary for your organization to create better interfaces consistently.   While it takes a great deal of work to get this process
started and to keep it working, the results will be worth the effort.
In the next few paragraphs I will describe each of these six steps in
more detail.

OBTAIN THE SUPPORT OF MANAGEMENT

Setting up the policies and procedures needed to produce effective
interfaces and keep them in place requires the commitment of a
wealth of resources.   These resources include skilled personnel
spending a substantial amount of time managing the interface process, especially when the process is being established. This will not
happen unless management is willing to commit these resources.
This commitment requires that management do at least the following:

- Assign skilled, experienced people.
- Release these people from their other commitments.
- Set up a system of rewards to provide the technical staff with the incentive to produce better interfaces.

Quality people are every organization's scarcest resource. They are always busy with tasks important to management. These people are needed to establish the process to manage interface development. In order to get these people working on the problem, management must believe that creating better interfaces is an important goal for the organization. I cannot give you any magic formula for getting the attention of management, but I have found that many organizations are willing to make this commitment because they now recognize the importance of the interface to the success of their software. But often management realizes that they do know how to go about improving the interfaces to their products. One of the objectives of this book is to provide a place to start.

Once management is ready to make the commitment to producing effective interfaces, then you are already over the biggest hurdle. What is needed next is the assignment of good people who will be responsible for establishing the process of managing interface development. I recommend that you form a user-interface management team to set up and implement the remaining steps of this process. Why a team? There are two reasons: (1) the skills required to make this management process work come from several different talented disciplines, and (2) the people who will ultimately implement the interface management process, namely the software designers, need to participate in its establishment. To be effective, an interface management process cannot be imposed from above.

The quality of the people who are assigned to the team will be the first indication of the degree of commitment of management. It is critical that two types of people be assigned:

- People who have knowledge and experience in the process of interface development
- People who are important enough in your organization to make the process work

The team must include one or more people who are human factors experts in interface design or its equivalent. Experience in this area is critical. As you will see below, merely reading the literature is not enough. If you do not have such a person on your staff, you should consider either hiring someone who has the experience or obtaining the services of a consultant. As you will see from the activities described in this and the next chapter, you will have no trouble finding work for a full-time human factors specialist.

In addition to the human factors expert, you should have a writer on the team. The writer, an important member of the development team, will be responsible for the documentation — both on-line and on paper. Documentation is a critical component of your product. In fact, the human factors expert and the writer are the two people who are most likely to view the product from the user's point of view. These two specialists need to work closely together. The writer should be responsible for creating and editing all of the online documentation including menu wording, messages, help, and tutorials.

Other important people the team should include are members of your software development organization, such as requirements and systems analysts, software engineers, programmers, and quality assurance specialists. Initiating a set of software interface practices takes a cooperative effort. In addition you may also want to add an expert in human testing to handle issues that require empirical testing.

Ideally, you should also have a user representative on your team. For example, if you are developing a product for a hospital environment, put a nurse on your team either on a full-time basis or as a consultant. Having a user representative with you as you make your day-to-day decisions will help you to create more usable products. Remember, however, that as user representatives work with you over a period of months or years, they can no longer see the product as a new user would. Consequently, putting a user representative on your team does not eliminate the need for the prototyping and usability testing described later in this chapter.

Once these people are assigned to the development team, they will have to meet regularly to carry out the remaining steps in the process. Depending on the goals you set for your team, you may have to meet every week until you have completed your user-interface handbook and educated your staff in its use. Some people on the team will have to spend more time. If you have a human factors specialist on your team, he or she may have to be dedicated to this work full-time for several months. Efforts such as this either gather their own momentum or fizzle and die. If an organization is willing to get the interface development management process started, it should also be willing to commit the staff needed to do it.

A critical component in managing interface development is to provide an incentive to produce better interfaces. The incentive must apply not only to the members of the team, but also to the product development staff producing the software. Whatever process your organization uses for performance and salary review, it must also include the quality of the employee's work in the creation of user interfaces. Software designers who consistently employ good practices in their work and who actively cooperate to improve these practices should be rewarded with salary increases and, most importantly, it should be made clear to them that their interface work has contributed to their increase. On the other hand, software designers who continually violate good practices and/or refuse to cooperate in the improvement of these practices should be told during their review that their user-interface work is not satisfactory.

In order for the interface development management to be effective, members of the team and management must understand that establishing a set of procedures to produce better interfaces is an educational process. As I will show, creating guidelines and imposing them on the software development staff is not likely to work. Your user-interface specialists must work with these people so that they come to understand the principles of interface design and your user-interface specialists come to understand the constraints under which they work.

SET ACHIEVABLE GOALS

The first and most important task for you and your user interface management team is to set reasonable goals. In my experience, some organizations fail to get started on the road toward improving their user interfaces because they want to achieve too much, too quickly and are overwhelmed by the process. You must be realistic. It is rare when an organization can start from scratch without any constraints and gain the full cooperation of its staff. If your organization is like most that I have seen, you will face at least two constraints as you begin the process of managing user-interface development.

First, you have existing finished products that incorporate practices that you may want to keep using. Some of these products may even have procedures and formats that you feel are part of your identity to your users or customers. You may want to keep these practices even though they are not optimum. I would, of course, recommend that you seriously consider changing any feature of the interface that will make the product better for the user. Every design, however, is a compromise among conflicting goals and sometimes the quality of the user interface loses to some other goal that is seen as more important. You or your user-interface management team must decide which of your established practices are not to be changed and which ones can be. Over time, as you gain more experience, you may want to reevaluate this decision, but it is important to set your boundaries in order to get started.

Second, your software developers are likely to resist major changes to existing practice. In many organizations, "existing practice" means that software designers do whatever they feel is new or innovative. Any constraints that are put on what the designers feel is an expression of their creativity will be vehemently resisted. You will have to introduce changes slowly and with care. In this chapter and the next, I will present some ways to expedite this process. The point here is that staff resistance is likely to be a problem that you will have to overcome. Staff resistance can be overcome, but you must be ready to face it if you expect to get the interface development process started.

A reasonable goal for your organization might be to focus first on a single new product at the beginning of its development cycle. Then, try to create a user interface to that product that users find acceptable and one that does not violate the basic principles described in Chapter 4. Don't try to regulate every word, format, or procedure of the product, but do require that your staff follow a well-defined set of basic guidelines and rules. After the product is developed you can set new goals, expand the guidelines, and apply your experience to other products.

CREATE A USER-INTERFACE HANDBOOK

One of the critical steps in the establishment of a process to manage interface development is the creation of a document that everyone in your organization can use as a base line. Section II of this book is intended to provide the foundation for such a base line. I recommend that you create a user-interface handbook for your organization, using the guidelines described in that section. The handbook should contain the guidelines, rules, and practices that your design staff should follow. The next chapter will show you how to create the handbook, how to tailor the guidelines in Section II of this book to the special needs to your organization, and how to present the guidelines in a form that your staff can apply directly to their work.

In addition to creating a handbook, the user interface management team will have to define its policies on how the guidelines and rules in the handbook will be implemented. In particular, there are two policy issues you must make clear to your software development staff:

1.   How will the guidelines and rules in the handbook be enforced? The users of the handbook, in this case the software engi-

neers, need to know who will verify that they have complied with the guidelines and rules and how this verification will be performed.

2. How will deviations from the handbook be handled? There should be some mechanism that allows software designers to try out new ideas that deviate from the handbook in some way.

It is important to define these policies before the handbook is distributed so that the software design staff will know in advance who will be responsible for interpreting the guidelines and the degree of flexibility they will have for exploring new ideas. My advice here is to

1. Assign someone, preferably a human factors specialist, to be responsible for enforcing the guidelines for each product under development. This person will be responsible for verifying that the handbook is being followed. When disputes arise, the issue can be arbitrated by someone, such as the project manager, who will have the final word.

2. Provide a waiver mechanism that encourages the exploration of new ideas. For instance, a waiver form could be included in the handbook that allows any software engineer with an innovative technique to at least prepare a prototype for testing. As I will show in the next chapter, it is important to make it clear in your handbook that its objective is not to stop the development of creative approaches, but rather to eliminate poor practices and to provide consistency in the interface to the user.

If you spend some time explaining these policies before the guidelines are distributed, their implementation will proceed more smoothly.

EMPHASIZE THE INTERFACE THROUGHOUT THE SOFTWARE DEVELOPMENT PROCESS

Over the past twenty years, there has been a major shift in the method by which software is developed. It began with structured programming, then moved backward through the development process to structured design, and then to structured requirements analysis. In addition to these techniques, most organizations now hold formal reviews throughout the development process. Sometimes these reviews are called structured walkthroughs. These structured development methods were created to make programs easier to maintain. Before structured techniques, a large percentage, perhaps sixty to eighty percent, of the life-cycle cost of software occurred after the program was coded. The debugging, testing, and maintenance of software consumed most of the resources in a software development organization. Modern structured techniques, when properly applied, produce more efficient software that can in turn be more easily maintained.

Notice, however, that structured software development techniques do not speak directly to the user interface. The classic text on structured design, Yourdon and Constantine's *Structured Design*, never mentions the user interface, nor do many contemporary texts on software design (Casel 1983; King 1984; Martin and McClure 1985; Higgins 1986). Even the literature that stresses the practice of having users attend product reviews does so from the point of view of functionality. The emphasis in this literature is on whether the software meets the user's requirements by getting the job done, not on how easy it is to learn and use.

If you intend to improve your user-software interfaces, you must put special emphasis on them throughout the software development process. There are four activities that I have found to be especially critical:

1. Define the requirements for the interface. It is beyond the scope of this book to describe the methods to be used to conduct requirements analyses. Each organization has its own preferred method. What is important is that you pay special attention to the user interface in addition to the functionality of the product during the early stages of the requirements process, and that you have a separate section of your requirements documentation devoted to the user interface. You should also consider creating a user interface specification along with your other specifications. This specification will emphasize the importance of the interface to the readers and provide you with easy access to the interface requirements during the development process.

Defining the requirements for the interface is just as important as defining the requirements for the other components of the software. During the requirements definition stage, someone should be assigned the responsibility for developing the requirements for the user interface. A human factors specialist can be very helpful here.

Human factors specialists can play a critical role during the requirements analysis stage of product development by ensuring that the functionality of the product and its ease of use meet user needs. These specialists are not only trained to view products from the user's point of view, but they are also trained in methods for gathering requirements from people. Some of these methods, such as systematic observation and focus groups, provide detailed information on the behavior, attitudes, and opinions of people; other methods, such as survey questionnaires, provide less detailed information but from a broader sampling of people. By applying these methods during the requirements stage of product development, the human factors specialist can help to identify who the potential users are, what technical and computer skills they have, and what the functions are that the product needs to be successful.

The process by which you gather information to develop requirements is frequently a function of the goal of your software development effort. If your organization is developing the software for another unit or division of your own company, then you can go directly to the end users in that unit to gather your information. On the other hand, if you are producing software to sell outside of your company, there is no readily available group of users from which you can gather information.

When you go to the users in the target unit, you will need to gather information that clearly establishes (1) the level of skill and experience of the end users with computers; (2) how they will use the product to help them to do their jobs; and (3) the constraints imposed by the environment in which the product will be used. You will need to answer such questions as

- Who are the users and how many of them are there?
- What technical skills do they possess?
- How do they do their jobs now?
- What services do their jobs perform?
- What product functions could help them to do their jobs better or faster?
- Are there situations when they are under stress or time pressure? Are there special demands that these situations will place on the product?
- Have they ever used a computer before?
- Will they know the basics of using software, such as how to use menus, or how to press the RETURN key after each entry?
- Will some of them be experienced users who demand speed and shortcuts in the software?
- Will the software be used on a daily basis by the same people or infrequently by a variety of people?

These are only some of the questions that you will need to ask. The answers to these questions will provide you with the information needed to make some basic decisions, such as which methods should be used to control the transactions between the software and the user (See Chapter 5.), and whether such features as "New User Help" or a tutorial will be needed. (See Chapter 8.)

If your organization intends to market the software being developed, the requirements definition process is more difficult. Often you will be given only vague statements from your marketing people such as "...this product is intended for experienced engineers and their managers..." or "... the target population has some experience with software... ." If these are the types of statements given to you by marketing, then you must clearly and specifically define the skills and experience of the intended user population. You must eliminate vague terms such as "some experience" and "computer literate" and substitute phrases such as "...logs in to a computer at least once a month..." or ". . .have used a word processor on a daily basis... ." A human factors specialist can help here by gathering data from potential users and by conducting usability tests as early as possible in the development cycle.

You can never know enough about users and how they do their work. Unfortunately, understanding users is costly and time-consuming. Therefore, defining the scope of your information gathering about users is critical (Dumas 1986). If you don't collect enough data about users, you run the risk of designing a product that does not help them. If you collect too much data, you may overrun your budget. Faced with this dilemma, most organizations choose to collect less data — an amount insufficient to understand potential product users. Most often they make this decision without the advice of a human factors specialist. An experienced human factors specialist can help the product development team to schedule, budget, and execute data collection methods that gather enough relevant data to define the requirements for the functionality of the product as well as its user interface.

The problem of deciding how much data to collect about users is especially difficult when the product being designed does not automate an already existing manual process, but rather provides users with new capabilities that they never had before, capabilities that change the way they work. In this case, understanding in great detail how users currently do their jobs may not provide all of the information you need to understand the problems they might have with the new product. Furthermore, users may not be much help to you in these situations. Frequently, users are resistant to accepting a process that changes what they now do. They may not understand your vision of how the product will make their jobs easier or more productive, or make the products of their effort better. In these situations you have no choice but to pursue your vision. Designing for the user does not mean that you have to accept at face value everything they say to you. It does mean that you make every effort to view the product from their point of view and that you gather any data you need to accomplish this goal. You will also have to conduct the usability tests described later in this chapter to confirm that your vision is accurate.

2. Prototype the interface. At the end of the requirements phase or early in the design phase, you should create a prototype of the interface to the product you are developing. The prototype can be as simple as a paper copy of the screens. With modern prototyping software, however, it is quick and easy to create screen formats. If you can go further than this and put some interactivity in the screens, do so. The closer your prototype comes to the final end product, the better your review with the users will be. This includes creating the actual environment that the users will eventually experience. If possible, use the hardware and the communications rate that they will be using when the product is complete. A product can look very good when you show it in a development environment at a fast communications rate, but then look quite poor in a realistic environment at a slower communications rate.

The prototype will also assist your software designers with their detailed design work. However, its greatest asset is that it allows you and your users to see, for the first time, what the finished product will look like. Often it is only when users see the displays that they really begin to think about how they want the software, and therefore the interface, to work for them. Commenting on the prototype also allows users to participate in the design, which has been shown to increase their satisfaction with the product and the use of it after it is operational (Baroudi, Olson, and Ives 1986).

The prototype is usually the first opportunity to determine whether the software designers are following the guidelines and rules in the user-interface handbook. You or your user-interface specialist should review the interface at this time for conformity to good user-interface practice. Then, provide feedback to your software designers about any deviations from these practices which reduce the effectiveness of the interface. The prototype is not the finished product, so being picky will not help anyone at this point. It is important, however, to open up the dialogue about the interface as early as possible. The prototype provides the first opportunity.

3. Review the interface early and often. The review of the prototype often provides the first opportunity to review the user interface design. Most organizations, however, hold several other re-

views throughout the development cycle. If your organization does not have formal reviews, it is essential that you find a way to meet with your software people to talk about their design for the interface. I believe you will find that they will not understand or appreciate the principles of interface design until you and/or your human factors expert sit with them at reviews and provide comments about their interface. It is only by talking about specific decisions they have made that they begin to understand the user's point of view. At the same time, the designers will have an opportunity to explain their decision-making process to you, including the constraints they believe they have. This dialogue will help each of you to understand the other's point of view. Many of the most difficult design decisions require complex tradeoffs between conflicting goals. I will have more to say about these tradeoffs in Section II. I can say here, however, that many software people are now more sophisticated about interfaces than they were a few years ago. The mistakes occurring now result less from neglecting the users than from focusing too much on one goal, or from forgetting about an important guideline while focusing on another. For this reason it is more effective to supplement guidelines by working directly with the designers throughout the software development process.

4.   Emphasize the interface in your quality control procedures. Strictly speaking, much of what I have been describing in this chapter is quality control. Many people, however, restrict the meaning of "quality control" to the verification testing of the software that is done near the end of development. The degree of formality of this testing varies from organization to organization.   Whichever way your organization conducts its verification testing, it is important to ensure that the testing of the interface has a recognized place in the testing process.   Remember, the testing phase may be your last opportunity to make changes before the product is released.

CONDUCT USABILITY TESTS

Experience has shown that predicting the usability of a product from inspection of its interface is as difficult as predicting the performance of a computer program from an inspection of its code. The interaction of computers and people is too complex to understand without the aid of empirical testing (Schell 1986). You would never accept the validity of a process to verify a computer program that did not include running the program with test cases and checking the results. Similarly, you should not accept claims for the usability of a product unless it has been empirically tested for usability.

"Usability testing" refers to testing that occurs when potential users are brought into a controlled environment, given access to the software and the documentation that goes with it, and asked to perform tasks for which the software was designed. Usability testing is not just a verification technique. It is a critical part of the software development process. The earlier you can begin exposing your product to users, the better the final results will be. As soon as you have a piece of the product functioning, bring in users to try it out. Then, observe closely their reactions and make changes accordingly.

Conducting usability tests is the only way to be sure, before the product is released, that the user interface design and documentation have achieved their goals. There is no substitute for a good usability test. It will provide an objective evaluation of a software product and its documentation. If the products your organization is producing are to be sold, it is very important that you set up a formal usability testing program. You do not have the advantage of having the users of your software within your organization.

A good way to think about the importance of usability testing in the development of a product is to consider the development of the interface as a two-stage process. The first stage consists of all of those activities that lead up to the usability test — defining requirements, creating a user-interface handbook, prototyping and reviewing the interface, etc. The objective of these activities is to minimize the changes that will have to be made as a result of testing. The second stage consists of the usability tests and the changes that are made as a result of the testing. You can be sure that there will be changes. By identifying these changes early, you will save the time and money you would have to spend correcting them later.

It is important that you encourage your software development team to observe the usability tests or a video tape of them. By doing so they will begin to understand why users have problems with software. In fact, usability tests have such a dramatic impact on the people who watch them, that you may want to initiate your user-interface development program with a usability test. You avoid most of the early resistance to new practices by providing an objective example that shows that the existing practices are not working as well as they should. Perhaps the most important outcome of usability testing, other than making the product better, is that it teaches a design team respect for users. Watching an obviously intelligent user sitting confused before the screen, you gain an appreciation for users that you didn't have before. Users become real people rather than faceless abstractions.

Usability tests can also help when you are considering the use of new interface-design features. The guidelines described in Section II of this book will not provide you with all the answers to your interface design questions. Note also that one of Murphy's Laws of human factors is that you can never find an empirical study that provides an answer to the specific question you have. Furthermore, the published studies always lag behind the technology. Consequently, you will often find yourself in the position of not knowing whether a major feature you are considering will, in fact, be effective. Even if you or some other member of your organization is convinced a new technique will work, it is vital that you settle these issues by subjecting them to an empirical test. Exposing your alternatives to a few test subjects is far safer than relying on someone's guess or on the opinion of the person with the strongest personality. Empirical testing needs to become part of your overall management strategy for the development of your products. It not only allows you to make better design decisions, but also makes you more sophisticated in the way in which you think about interfaces and about the skills of your users.

Product managers sometimes resist efforts to test because they believe it will keep them from completing the product on schedule and within budget. While it is true that successful testing does require the time of several people, such as a test director, a hardware engineer, and a software engineer, these costs are well worth it because they can reduce the life cycle cost of the product. Releasing an untested product can lead to frustration and anger with the product, which can reduce sales. It can also result in added costs for the extra training and support staff needed to help customers deal with a clumsy interface.

While testing may add costs to development, it does not have to add much extra time. Testing can be done in an iterative fashion in parallel with other activities. As pieces of the product are designed, they can be tested while other development activities continue. A final test of the completed product may add a couple of weeks to the development schedule.

One way to minimize the costs of testing is to plan your tests carefully. While this is not a book on testing, I can give you some guidance that may help you avoid the major pitfalls. The first step in conducting a usability test is to require the person who is responsible for the test, the test manager, to create a test plan. This will ensure that critical issues are considered before each test. The plan does not have to be lengthy, but it should encompass the following:

- The test objective
- The test subjects
- The test measures
- The data analysis

The Test Objective

Each test should have a clearly stated objective. Preferably, the objective should be stated in terms of the performance of the test subjects. For example, "The objective of this test is to determine whether the creating and editing of a document can be done faster with a mouse than with a digitizing tablet." Try to avoid vague concepts such as making subjects "more comfortable" or "more productive." If the objective of the test actually is to find what users prefer, state the objective in terms of the subject's rating, for example, "The objective of this test is to determine whether menu selection by mouse is rated easier to use than selection by keying a number."

The Test Subjects

The number and type of test subjects needed for a test is one of those issues that causes endless debate. Be assured that there is no "right" answer to this question. The test manager must decide how to balance the cost, in time and resources, of running the test against the potential importance of the outcome of the test. There are, however, some guidelines you can use to make your decisions. First, determine how many categories of potential users there are. For example, if the product is intended for both new and experienced computer users, you will need to sample from both populations. Once you determine the number of categories, you must then decide how to sample within these categories. My advice is to select both people that you consider "typical" in each of the categories and people that you consider to be at the extremes of the population. For example, if your potential user population includes project managers, you might select new and experienced project managers who have (1) occasionally used a computer, (2) never used a computer, and (3) have personal computers at home.

Once you have decided on the types of subjects you need, you must then decide how many subjects to test. Again, there is no "right" answer to this question. Sometimes one subject is enough to send you back to the drawing board. I have found that five to fifteen subjects is enough to uncover the major problems with a user interface. Remember, you normally are testing the interface to uncover features that make a difference in the user's performance and preference. These features should be obvious to you after testing a few subjects.

In certain situations, it may be useful to have more than one user attend a test. In cases where the objective is to help make design decisions, perhaps among competing alternatives, rather than just verifying the effectiveness of the decisions you have made, having two subjects who interact with each other can provide you with a rich description of reactions to your screens and procedures. Using two subjects in a test is sometimes called the "co-discovery" method. It works best when you do not give the subjects extensive training or information. Simply give them the minimum instructions they will need to get started and then give them tasks to perform. For example, if you were testing a product for a hospital environment, you might bring in two nurses and ask them to transfer a patient from one room to another. I have found that it helps if the two people know each other and if you encourage them to "think out loud." You will be amazed at the amount of information you will get out of these sessions. The subjects will talk to each other about what the words on the screen mean to them and why they think they ended up on the wrong screen or used the wrong procedure. I have frequently found it a humbling experience to attend these sessions and to see how a design I have worked hard on can lead the user astray. On the other hand, these sessions can also give you a confident feeling that you understand how to make the interface more effective.

The Test Measures

There are two broad categories of measures that are usually gathered during a test involving human subjects: performance measures and subjective judgments. Performance measures are variables such as speed and accuracy. Subjective measures usually include ratings and opinions expressed in an interview or questionnaire. Performance measures will provide you with objective data. Gather them whenever you can. You do not need to have elaborate equipment or specialized software to make such measurements. A simple stop watch or a tape recorder and a scoring sheet on which an observer records performance is often enough. In most cases you will also want to collect subjective measures. Whenever possible, use a face-to-face interview instead of a self-administered questionnaire to gather this data. Good questionnaires are difficult to create. Construct an interview guide to help structure your interview and make your questions as specific as possible. For example, if your test objective is to assess the user's preference for a feature you are testing, ask for a numerical rating.

You should also tape record your test sessions so that you do not have to write down everything the test subject says. The tape will also provide you with data on the time that events occurred. You do not always need to videotape your test sessions to measure the effectiveness of the software or the documentation. The primary value of video taping is to illustrate dramatically the key responses of users to your product. Videotaping, however, will not always help to evaluate the product. You cannot tape the actions of the test subject, the screen display, and the documentation with one camera. You would be amazed at how difficult it is to figure out what a test subject is doing from watching a video tape made with one camera. If you have a multiple camera facility, you may want to tape the session to show your software staff, your management, or other key people. To do so, you will have to spend time editing the tape to cut out the long stretches when nothing happens. Such a demonstration tape may not provide you with much help in evaluating the software or the documentation, but it may provide you with a tool to show key people the highlights of the test.

The Data Analysis

While you are planning your test, create hypothetical data that could result from the measures you have decided to use. Then ask yourself what conclusions you would draw from this data. This exercise will help you to avoid that sinking feeling that occurs when the test is completed, and you then realize the data provided did not accurately test your objective.

In conclusion, if you spend a little time planning your test, you can avoid making major mistakes. In addition to the planning, you should also try out your test procedures before you test your first subject. Don't make the first subject work out the bugs in your test procedures for you.

KEEP YOUR HANDBOOK UP-TO-DATE

Your user-interface handbook should be a living document. When you first create it, it will help you begin to produce better interfaces. As you acquire some experience using the guidelines and rules in it, however, you will see that they need improvement. You may also find that the handbook does not cover new technologies and new interaction techniques that become available. Periodically you must update your handbook to improve it and keep it current with the latest techniques that your software development staff is using. It is important that your handbook not lose credibility by being partially out of date.

There are several sources of feedback that you can use to keep your handbook current:

- Interface reviews. As you work with the handbook you will find that some of your guidelines are unclear or are misleading. In addition, you will accumulate examples of good and poor interface practices.   Incorporate these examples into your handbook and improve any guidelines that are not clear to others.
- Test results. Your test program will provide you with valuable information about problems potential users are having with the interfaces your organization is producing.   When you find something useful from your test program, incorporate it into your handbook.
- The human factors literature. Keep abreast of the new research and thinking of the human factors community.   The following periodicals and proceedings frequently contain articles on various aspects of the user interface:

Computer
Communications of the ACM
Datamation
Ergonomics
International Journal of Man-Machine Studies
Human Factors
Proceedings of the ACM Subgroup on Human-Computer Interaction
Proceedings of the Human Factors Society

Check these sources regularly for new information and incorporate it into your handbook.

In order to facilitate frequent updating of your handbook, you may want to consider keeping it in machine-readable form. This practice will allow you to avoid continually putting out paper addendums to your handbook or having to republish it when there are only a few changes. It may also make the handbook more acceptable to the software development staff. When you put it on the computer, it somehow becomes more like "software" than just another paper report. You may also want to index it and provide an online query capability that will allow your staff to look up a rule online while they are working on a product.

Chapter 3

*Creating
a User-Interface
Handbook*

OVERVIEW

A user-interface handbook is a vehicle through which the members of a design team understand the practices they should follow to create effective products. It is a working document meant to be used on a daily basis and modified as needed. It should contain all of the information needed to design the user interface. The guidelines and local conventions are the core of the handbook, but it can also contain such items as commonly used modules and a glossary of terms to be used in the interface design.

To create a handbook you will need to decide on the scope of practices you want to improve, select the guidelines from Section II that apply to those practices, translate the guidelines into local rules if possible, and add examples and new guidelines that apply to your special needs.

The handbook should be developed with the help of all of the members of the design team. It should not be so specific that it presents a barrier to the exploration of creative new practices.

In the last chapter, I described a management process that you can establish in your organization to begin to create more effective products. One of the key steps in that process is the development of a user-interface handbook. The handbook is the vehicle through which the members of the design team understand the guidelines and conventions they should follow and the importance of designing with the user in mind.

You might reasonably ask why I haven't created such a handbook instead of writing this book. The answer is that this book is intended to apply to any organization creating software. As a consequence, I can only describe guidelines that everybody can use. To implement these guidelines, you will have to translate some of them into local rules that you and your team can follow. For example, in several of the chapters on guidelines, I recommend that users should be able to leave a menu or a data entry screen or a lengthy help message at any time. In order to implement these guidelines, you and your design team must decide specifically which procedure users will follow to leave these screens, such as with a particular function key. I cannot tell you in this book what that procedure will be. I can tell you only that you need one and provide you with examples of some procedures which might be effective and some which might not. You must decide on the procedure and put it in your handbook. As I will show in this chapter, not all of the guidelines need to be translated, but many do. This book provides the foundation for your handbook, but you must make the guidelines applicable to your organization's needs.

You may also find that the guidelines in Section II do not apply to some of the decisions you have to make in the design of a new product. User-interface guidelines are simply a convenient way to express the accumulated knowledge of the community of people who study human-computer interaction on how to design effective interfaces. Many of the guidelines are based on empirical research; others are based on practical design experience. If you are using new man-machine interface technology or are using established technology in a new way, you will find situations where the guidelines do not help. In those cases, you will have to make a decision about what you think will work and then conduct usability tests to verify your decision. As a result of testing, you may be able to create new guidelines to add to your handbook.

I have chosen the word "handbook" to describe the document I believe you should create because I want to convey the message that it is both a working document and a living one. It is meant to be used on a daily basis rather than read once and put on a shelf. Further, it should be modified and updated as you introduce new technologies and as research about human-computer interaction adds to our knowledge of how to design better products. The handbook is not intended to restrict the creativity of your design team, but rather to ensure that every team member knows which good practices to use and which poor ones to avoid.

In this chapter I will describe

- The need for a handbook
- How to create one
- What the handbook should contain
- How to avoid restricting creativity and exploration of new ideas

THE NEED FOR A HANDBOOK

The fact that the user interface to many products is poor indicates that many software designers and programmers are having difficulty creating effective interfaces. These designers and programmers need to know which practices to apply to improve their products, and all of the members of the development team need to follow the same set of rules and guidelines. An effective way to achieve this consistency is to create a user-interface handbook that describes these practices. Before looking at how to create the handbook, look

Figure 3-1   A User-Interface Handbook can improve consistency

at what happens when there are no rules that everyone agrees to follow.

For the past few years I have been keeping a list of the exit terms and procedures I encounter as I use and evaluate software. The list as it now stands appears at the top of page 37.

You may recognize many of these terms. Some of them, such as "QUIT," are frequently used in menus, while others, such as "LO," are used in command languages. I have found several of these procedures in the same product. For example, one product I evaluated used "BYE," "QUIT," and "99" as exit procedures.

```
BYE          LOGOUT
CLOSE        Q
E            QUIT
EN           SIGNOFF
END          SYSTEM
EX           X
EXIT         CONTROL A
FINISH       CONTROL C
LEAVE        CONTROL Y
KILL         CONTROL Z
K/A          0
K/F          99
LO           999
```

There are two notable features of this list. The first is its length. There are over twenty-five terms listed here. You may know of even more. Given the size of this list, you can see that programmers have many options from which to choose when deciding something as simple as an exit procedure. Second, not all of the terms in the list are effective ways to describe how to leave a screen. Terms such as "quit," "exit,"and "end" have meanings that can make their use as ways to describe leaving a screen or a program intuitively clear. The meaning of some of the other items in the list, however, is not as clear. For example, "LO" makes sense only as an exit procedure if you understand that it is an abbreviation for "LOGOUT." Furthermore, you must also know that "LOGOUT" usually means to terminate communications, not only with the application, but also with the computer. Some of the other terms have no obvious connection to exiting at all. For example, you may recognize the command used to exit from some versions of BASIC, namely, "SYSTEM." "99" and "999" are classic examples of a programmer's use of an exit procedure that makes sense only if you know the logic of the code. They make no sense to the user as exit procedures. It is clear that of the many choices that programmers have for an exit procedure, some are better than others.

This example is only one of many I could have chosen to illustrate the need for a user-interface handbook. Members of the software design team need guidance when they are creating an interface. They need to know what practices they should follow and what conventions the other designers are using.

It is important for you to realize that you cannot just have members of your design team read a book such as this one and expect them to know how to implement its guidelines. Furthermore, when new programmers join your organization or your product development team, they will bring with them their own set of words, formats, and procedures that they have acquired through their training and experience. Each programmer's training and experience are different. In order to create effective interfaces, all team members need to follow the same good practices. Otherwise, you run the risk of using practices that will confuse and frustrate users. An effective way to avoid inconsistencies and poor practices is to identify in a handbook those practices you and your team will follow.

HOW TO CREATE A HANDBOOK

Creating a user-interface handbook is not difficult. Given the benefits of having one, it is surprising that more organizations have not written down the conventions that they want to follow. One of the reasons that this does not happen more often is that most organizations have not set up a user-interface management process. Without such a process, attempts to regulate the development of the interface are difficult to initiate.

To create an effective handbook, I recommend that you

- Set achievable goals for the practices you want to regulate
- Select the guidelines that apply to those practices
- Create new guidelines when they are needed
- Translate any guidelines that you can into local rules
- Add examples that are relevant to your products

1. Set achievable goals for your handbook. I made the point in the last chapter that you must set achievable goals for your user-interface management process. The goals should constrain your objectives for the handbook. If you try to regulate all aspects of the interface in one step, you are likely to be overwhelmed by the process. In order to get started, focus on the design areas that are most important to you and your products. For example, you may decide that your most pressing need is for an effective online help system.

2. Select the guidelines that apply. Once you decide which aspects of the interface you want to regulate, select the relevant guidelines from Section II. For example, if you decide to develop online help, use the guidelines in Chapter 8 as an initial starting point for your handbook.

3. Add new guidelines when they are needed. You may want to supplement the guidelines in this book with others that you find useful. The most complete compilation of guidelines is contained in a series of reports published by the MITRE Corporation for the Air

Force. The most recent of these is Smith and Mosier (1986). You may also add your own guidelines that result from testing new features that apply to your product line.

4. Translate guidelines into local conventions whenever you need to. As I have shown in this chapter, some guidelines are not specific enough to allow everyone on your team to apply them in the same manner. Exit procedures are a good example. There has to be some consensus among all the members of the team, however, so that they all use the same procedure. This is one of the primary functions of the handbook. It allows you to translate guidelines into specific conventions that are tailored to your organization and your products. Formats, the mapping of function keys, entry and exit procedures, terminology, symbology, and the wording of status messages and options are areas where local conventions are needed to provide programmers with specific rules to follow. These conventions are necessary to achieve consistency within and across your products.

Not all guidelines can be translated into specific organizational conventions. Generally, you can standardize such features as the words that are used in the interface, screen formats, function key mappings, and simple procedures. You cannot create a rule that tells programmers how to write every error or help message. You can give them guidelines to follow, such as to be specific in describing the cause of an error, but you can't create a rule that will tell them how to write every message. Remember that guidelines are important even if you cannot translate them into specific conventions because guidelines state important goals to be achieved. Throughout Section II, I have indicated when guidelines need to be translated into local rules.

5. Add examples to make your guidelines and conventions clear. In Section II there are many examples that illustrate how to interpret and apply the guidelines. You should supplement these examples with ones that are relevant to your products. It is difficult for many programmers to translate guidelines and principles that may seem, and sometimes are, ambiguous into specific actions. You need to provide examples to help them understand what the words in a guideline mean for them.

WHAT SHOULD THE HANDBOOK CONTAIN?

The guidelines and conventions that regulate the design of the user-interface are the core of the handbook. But the handbook can contain much more. Remember that it is meant to be used on a daily basis and to be added to and modified frequently. It should be the one source that contains all of the available information on user-interface design. It can contain such items as software modules or directories of modules that are already available to help to code the interface software.

There are two aids that I strongly recommend be part of your handbook. The first is a set of general principles of interface design, such as those described in Chapter 4. The principles provide the rationale for the guidelines. When programmers ask why a guideline is important to follow, the general principles provide an answer. Without them, the guidelines may appear to be unrelated rules.

A second aid is a glossary of terms. A glossary provides definitions of all the key words that are displayed on the screen as part of the user interface. It will prevent inconsistencies in wording, such as using "modify" and "update" to mean the same thing, and it will allow you and your staff to select words that convey the precise meaning that you want.

WILL THE HANDBOOK STIFLE CREATIVITY?

Some of the managers I talk with are reluctant to regulate any of the practices of their software staff. They feel that software design is a very creative process and that in the long run their products will become sterile and their staff will mutiny if rules are imposed.

I sympathize with this concern and agree that you could create a handbook that is so specific, comprehensive, and restrictive in the way it is enforced that it would do more harm than good. On the other hand, I do not believe that you are stifling the creativity of programmers because you create a rule requiring them to put a title on a menu or to use a word in the same way on two different screens, or to forbid them to write vague or insulting messages. Some standardization is absolutely essential if the interface is to be consistent and free of the worst abuses of good practice.

As you expand your standardization beyond the basics, you will have to consider whether the rules you are creating restrict the freedom of your design team too severely. One way to minimize this problem is to keep your software development team involved in decisions about what should be standardized and how.

You must continually reinforce the importance of the goal of creating more effective interfaces by designing from the user's point of view. If you show your team that you and your management are strongly committed to improving the interfaces to your products and if you also allow them to participate in usability tests of the product, they will be more willing to create the rules and to follow them. In addition, as I recommended in the last chapter, you need some form of waiver procedure that goes along with your handbook. If someone feels that they have a new technique or a better way to do things, let them try it out. Your usability tests will tell you whether the new technique makes any difference to the user's performance or satisfaction.

SECTION II

DESIGNING
THE INTERFACE

Over the years that I have been helping clients to design and evaluate software, I have frequently been asked at briefings such questions as: "What constitutes a good user interface?", or "How do I tell a good user interface from a poor one?" These are reasonable questions to ask, but they are not simple ones to answer. These questions can be approached from two levels. The first level is quite general and describes a good user interface as one that exhibits a set of broad principles, such as being consistent in wording, formats, and procedures. The second level is more specific and describes the practices that a designer should follow in creating an interface, such as placing meaningful titles on a menu or putting a blank line after every fifth row of a long list.

I have found that, when I speak only about broad principles in a typical hour briefing, the audience feels that I have simply described some goals to be achieved and have not told them how to achieve them. I have not told them specifically how to improve their products. On the other hand, if I speak about the specific rules and guidelines, the audience then feels that designing a user interface consists of following a random assortment of unrelated rules. I have not told them why the rules must be followed or how to organize them into meaningful groupings.

In this section I describe both levels. The general principles in the next chapter (Chapter 4) provide a framework that helps to structure the guidelines that follow and provide a rationale for them. The four subsequent chapters (Chapters 5-8) describe the guidelines that will make your user interface reflect the general principles. Each guideline attempts to communicate a rule in a few short words. The text that accompanies each guideline then elaborates on these words and frequently provides examples of both good and poor design practices to help interpret the guideline. Throughout these chapters there are also frequent references to relevant research studies that provide empirical data to justify the effectiveness of the guidelines.

Read the next chapter before you dig into the details of the guidelines that follow. The principles described there will help you interpret and organize the guidelines and will provide a rationale for why a particular guideline is important.

Chapters 5 through 8 contain the guidelines. They are organized into four areas: (1) controlling transactions, (2) displaying data, (3) entering data, and (4) smoothing communication with online documentation. This grouping is a relatively arbitrary one because some guidelines apply to more than one of these areas. This organization, however, will help you find guidelines that relate to a specific topic. For example, if you are looking for guidelines on Help messages, they will be found in Chapter 8 under online documentation.

The guidelines in these chapters represent a basic set of good user-interface practices. They are by no means an exhaustive set. You may want to supplement them with guidelines that apply to the specific design problems you encounter with your products. Remember that guidelines are a convenient way to communicate a set of practices that have worked successfully in the past. As new hardware and software technologies evolve, however, the guidelines that describe how to use them effectively will also change.

In addition, each guideline has a number assigned to it. The number contains two parts. The first part is the number of the chapter; the second part is the number of the guideline within the chapter. This means that guideline 6-1 is the first guideline in the sixth chapter. This numbering scheme will help you to cross-reference and to locate a guideline quickly. The Appendix contains a complete list of all of the guidelines and the page number where each appears.

Chapter 4

General Principles

OVERVIEW

You cannot mathematically derive an interface design from a set of equations. It is difficult to define the characteristics of an interface in rigorous terms. In the absence of an accepted theory, this chapter presents seven principles of interface design which together describe the characteristics of an effective interface. These principles also help to provide a rationale for the guidelines that follow in subsequent chapters. Each guideline contributes to one or more of the principles. To be consistent with the principles, your design should

- Put the user in control.
- Address the user's level of skill and experience.
- Be consistent.
- Protect the user from the inner workings of the hardware and software.
- Provide online documentation.
- Minimize the burden on the user's memory.
- Follow the principles of good graphics design.

The promotional literature for many new software products describes them as being "user-friendly" or "easy to learn and use." For the marketing professional, these words seem to summarize the qualities of an effective user interface. Do these phrases have any substantive meaning, however, for you as the designer of the interface? I believe they do have meaning, but it is not easy to convey this meaning in a few words.

Let's consider the term "user-friendly" for a moment. It has been used and abused many times and continues to be applied to user interfaces. Why? Because it carries a very powerful connotation. To say that software is "friendly" is to imply that it is like a human being, not just any human being, but one whom you know, feel comfortable with, and who knows you. A software product with these qualities would certainly be worth buying and using.

These phrases continue to be used in promotional literature because they fill a void caused by the lack of an accepted theory of human-computer interaction. The science of human-computer interaction is new and has often been called "soft" (Newell 1986). By "soft" I mean that it has no axioms, theorems, or equations as its foundation. You cannot derive an interface design mathematically from a set of equations. Interface designs can be rigorously evaluated and alternatives can be empirically tested, but a design cannot be computed from a basic theory. The present state of the science of human-computer interaction makes it difficult to define the characteristics of an interface in rigorous terms. Hence, the use of such terms as "user-friendly."

In the absence of a theory, we need some organizational concepts to tie together the guidelines and their derived rules of interface design. Seven principles are described here in an attempt to develop an organizing structure. These principles provide a set of general concepts to help you understand the importance of the guidelines that follow. For example, why is it important to display a status message, such as "Working," that keeps the user informed that the software is functioning normally? The answer, I believe, is that status messages contribute to the user's feeling of being in control of the software. Similarly, every guideline in this book is important to follow because each one contributes to one or more of the seven principles of good interface practice.

How have these principles been developed? They are derived from (1) my experience in creating, evaluating and thinking about interfaces, and (2) from the human factors literature. There are other authors who have proposed lists of general principles and some of these lists have principles similar to mine. While my principles may not be all-inclusive, they have been created to provide a foundation on which to build guidelines.

There is one aspect in which the principles described here are different from those presented by others. Many of the lists of principles in the software-interface literature are presented as if they had no relationship to guidelines, that is, the general principles and the specific guidelines are not related to each other. I have taken the principles one step further and related each principle to the guidelines that follow in subsequent chapters. The principles provide a rationale for the guidelines. This rationale is important because not every guideline is backed up by a research study showing that it makes a difference to the performance of users. Often, the only justification for a guideline is that it contributes to a more general principle that appears to be important. Consequently, tying the principles to the guidelines is a critical step to understanding why the guidelines should be followed.

As experience with new technologies and user-interface practices grows, I hope these principles will be refined and that they, in turn, will become part of a more general theory of human-computer interaction. For the present, I propose these principles as a tool to help relate the guidelines that follow to a broader context.

THE PRINCIPLES OF INTERFACE DESIGN

The subsequent sections of this chapter describe each of the seven principles of interface design:

- Put the user in control.
- Address the user's level of skill and experience.
- Be consistent.
- Protect the user from the inner workings of the hardware and software.
- Provide online documentation.
- Minimize the burden on the user's memory.
- Follow the principles of good graphics design.

These principles are roughly ordered based on their importance to the design of an effective interface. Since they have not been derived from a theory of human-computer interaction, there is no way to measure their relative importance. The principles at the top of the list, however, have a broader impact on the quality of a user interface than those at the bottom. Their ordering represents my best judgment of relative importance.

Included with the descriptions of each principle are indications of the relationship between the principle and the design guidelines in the following chapters.

■ Put the User in Control

I believe this principle is the most important. What does it mean? Making users feel they are in control has two components, a cognitive component and a behavioral component. The cognitive component means that the user understands the structure of the software interface and can predict its response to direction. I use the word "direction" here to refer to any means available to users that tells the software what they want to do, including menus, function keys, commands, etc. The behavioral component means that users know what actions they need to perform to accomplish tasks.

An effective interface allows users to (1) form an accurate and detailed cognitive representation of the structure of the software and to (2) learn quickly how to operate it. A poor interface does just the opposite. It frustrates and confuses users' attempts to understand it; it leaves users in constant doubt about where they are in the structure of the application; it makes users unsure that they can predict how the software will respond to their direction; it creates difficulties in operating the software; and it makes it easy to make errors but not to recover from them.

Because this is the broadest and most important principle, many of the practices that are described in the guidelines contribute to it, in one way or another. But the practices that contribute most to this principle are those that

- Provide online help that informs the user about the structure and operation of the application.
- Provide effective prompts and status messages that guide the user through procedures and keep them informed about program status.
- Provide error messages that allow the user to understand both what went wrong and how to smoothly recover from the error.
- Provide the user with the means to move freely within and between screens and the ability to move easily to major menus or nodes and to quickly exit from the application.
- Provide consistency in the use of words, formats and procedures.

■ Address the User's Level of Skill and Experience

Most software is created by people who are totally immersed in computer technology. Many have personal computers of their own and are familiar with the latest technological advances available. From their point or view, most applications do not come close to pushing the limits of the available technology.

On the other hand, most users are at the opposite end of the spectrum. While they may be familiar with an application area, their experience with computers can vary from none at all to having used a few basic applications, such as electronic mail. The percentage of people who have hands-on experience with computers is still very small. One of the most difficult problems for you as a software developer is overcoming this gap between your skills and the skills of most users. If the application you are developing will be used by people with virtually no computer experience, then your design must favor these users over the more experienced ones.

This does not mean, however, that you must ignore the needs of the more experienced users. They need a design that takes advantage of their experience. They should be able to take shortcuts and should be provided with online documentation that jogs their memory when they need it rather than a lengthy explanation of basics.

The practices that contribute most to this principle are those that

1. Avoid jargon. The interface must contain words, phrases, and examples that reflect the user's point of view, not that of the developer. All computer terms and other technical jargon not familiar to users must be eliminated from the interface or explained to the user. To meet this requirement adequately, a human factors specialist and technical writer should participate in and review the interface design for terminology a user may not understand. In addition, the design must be subjected to a usability test to ensure that potential users understand the words contained in menus, messages, help text, and tutorials.

2. Use appropriate transaction control procedures. The means by which users tell the software what they want to do must be compatible with their level of skill and experiences with computers. New users will be most comfortable with menus or simple question-and-answer dialogue. Experienced users can use these methods, but they may want to be able to string together sequences of commands and use function keys to speed up the operation of an application.

3. Provide several levels of detail for error and help messages. Experienced users need error and help messages to remind them of what they already know. New users, however, need step-by-step procedures and examples that instruct them in the operation of the application. The needs of both these groups can be met by providing more than one level of help and error messages. The first level should be short and provide the essential information. At this level the user then has the option of accessing and displaying subsequent levels that are more detailed.

■ Be Consistent in Wording, Formats, and Procedures

Consistency is an important feature that should be built into every interface and, wherever possible, it should be maintained across applications. Consistency helps the user to learn an application more easily, to use it more easily, and to recover more easily when there is a problem. In short, consistency is one of the factors that helps the user feel in control of the software.

No one with whom I have discussed interface guidelines has ever disagreed with this principle. In addition, every book, article, or speech on interface principles stresses consistency in one form or another. In fact, many people think that consistency is the primary goal of an effective interface design. I believe, however, that consistency, by itself, is not enough. You must use *good* practices consistently. In Chapter 3, I listed over twenty-five exit terms and procedures I have compiled over the past few years. One of the points I made about that list is that not all exit procedures used by programmers are good ones, even when they are used consistently. The fact that an application consistently uses "99" as an exit procedure does not make that a good practice. The key to an effective interface is to use good practices consistently.

Throughout the next four chapters I stress consistency by including a guideline on it near the end of each chapter or major section of a chapter. For example, Guideline 8-29 discusses the importance of consistency in the wording and format of help text. I chose this method rather than including a phrase such as "and do it consistently" at the end of each guideline.

I have included these guidelines to remind you about consistency. These guidelines, however, are not very specific; they simply state that consistency is important. As I have stressed in Chapters 2 and 3, an effective way to create better interfaces consistently is to prepare an organizational user-software interface handbook which you and your colleagues can follow. This handbook should contain the specific words, formats, and procedures that are to be employed consistently in the design of your products.

■ Protect the User from Inner Workings of the Hardware and Software that is Behind the Interface

The computer hardware we use to help us work and play in the 1980s is both powerful and flexible. The general purpose computer allows us to create an unlimited number of applications to meet our needs. To take advantage of this flexibility, however, we need applications software to harness the power of the computer. Application software itself is created using a more basic set of software tools.

When you create an application, you use such software tools as a high level language, system utilities, various libraries, and a database manager. These tools provide a buffer between you and the registers, memories, and other components of the hardware. Consequently, you do not have to deal with the details of machine operation directly.

When FORTRAN was created, its developers actually believed that it would eliminate the need for programming. Scientists, they believed, would simply write out their equations and the FORmula TRANslator would convert these equations into machine code. While these early developers were a bit optimistic in their expectations that FORTRAN would eliminate programming, they were correct in observing that it did provide a buffer between the programmer and the internal workings of the machine. The programmer was free to concentrate on the logic of the operations rather than worrying about such things as memory locations and registers.

You should provide a similar buffer between the end user and both the hardware components and the software tools you use to make the application run. One of the characteristics of a poor interface is that it displays information about the internal workings of the software that the typical end user cannot understand. For example, displaying a message such as "FORTRAN END" may tell you that the software is operating normally, but it may be meaningless to the end user. In addition, many new users are very sensitive about their lack of knowledge of computer hardware and software. As a consequence, they are immediately upset when words and phrases that describe the internal workings of the software are displayed on the screen. These words are intimidating because users assume that they should know what they mean. A good interface will protect the user from having to know about the inner workings of hardware and software tools in the same way that these tools protect you from having to deal with the internal details of the hardware and system software.

The practices that contribute most to this principle are those that

- Avoid jargon by using plain English rather than words and phrases that refer directly to the software tools you are using.
- Avoid displaying status messages such as "LINK MAIN" or "FORTRAN END." These messages describe the inner workings of the software in terms that the user cannot interpret.
- Avoid passing error messages generated by your software tools directly to the user. Translate them into plain English first and then display them to the user.

■ **Provide Online Documentation to Help the User to Understand How to Operate the Application and to Recover from Errors**

An extensive, well-designed, and well-written online help system has now become an accepted goal of many major software applications. Further, there is evidence that a well-designed help system improves the productivity of users and increases their satisfaction with a product (Magers 1983; Cohill and Willigies 1985). Users should not have to search continually through a shelf of manuals to make their way through an application. This is not to say that printed documentation does not have its place. Printed documentation is necessary to allow users to begin using an application. Once they have started, however, users should be able to complete most of their routine work with online documentation and, perhaps, a Quick Reference Guide.

The online documentation that users need consists of more than just online help messages. All messages that are displayed are part of the online documentation. As we will see in Chapter 8, status messages, prompts, and error messages are also components of online documentation. These messages inform users about the status of the operation of the application, and they help them to know how to proceed and how to recover from errors. In short, these messages are critical contributors to giving the user a sense of being in control.

The guidelines that contribute to this principle are those that describe the design of help, status, error messages, and prompts.

■ Minimize the Burden on the User's Memory

Human beings are notoriously poor at recalling detailed information but are remarkably good at recognizing it (McNulty 1965). In addition, the nature of the computer terminal screen puts an extra burden on users' memory. Unlike working with a printed document or even working on the top of a desk, a computer application typically consists of a sequence of screens that users can display in various orders. When one screen is displayed, the others cannot be seen. Even when the technology allows the screen to display multiple windows, there is a limit to how much information can be displayed and used at one time. Consequently, the user of a computer application is often forced to memorize information and to recall it later.

A good interface design should minimize the need for the user to memorize and later recall information. Whenever possible, users should be able to choose from lists and be allowed to use their recognition memory rather than their recall memory. The widespread acceptance of menus as a primary means to control the users' transactions with software is an example of an application of this principle.

There is more to minimizing memory load, however, than using menus. There are several other practices that also contribute to this principle:

1. Be consistent in your use of words, formats, and procedures. Consistency reduces the user's need to learn and remember new information. For example, when the same exit procedure is used on all menus, a user has to learn it only once and it is easier to remember.

2. Display status messages that remind users where they are in an application and what options are in effect. Simple status messages such as "Screen 2 of 3" and "F2 = Main Menu" reduce the

user's need to remember where they are in the application or what operations they can use to get where they want to go.

3.   Provide online help that is designed as an aid to memory. It is not only the new user who needs help to remember information. The experienced user also occasionally needs to be reminded about such items as how an infrequently used procedure works or the details of a data entry format. Online help that is designed as an aid to memory can provide this information so that experienced users can continue without having to search through their memory or a manual.

4.   Use memory joggers in prompts and data entry captions. For example, tell users how to format dates, such as (mm/dd/yy). Many of the details of formats and procedures are simply not important to the users of the information, so they quickly forget them. But these details are important to the software that stores and manipulates that information. One of the first things that new users learn about computers is that they must be careful about these details. A good interface design helps users with these details by including memory joggers in messages that request information.

■   **Follow Principles of Good Graphics Design in the Layout of Information on the Screen**

When you read a book or a magazine you expect that certain information layout practices will be followed: tables and figures will be centered on the page; columns in tables and lists will be justified properly; headings and subheadings will be informative and be in a consistent format. These practices are not important only because of their aesthetic nature. A tremendous amount of research has been done on the relationship between how information is displayed and how readers, both good and poor, process it. An analysis of this research indicates that there are principles of information display that help users to find what they want easily and to understand it. An effective interface must also follow these good information layout practices. Displays should be formatted so that the users can find what they want and read it with ease.

However, displaying information on a terminal screen imposes additional constraints on the design of layouts. A screen is substantially smaller than the pages of most documents. Also, the contrast on video screens is, in general, much poorer than the contrast available with printed documents. You cannot put as much information on a screen and keep it as legible as you can with most printed documents. Finally, most users will not read large blocks of text on a screen. For some reason, people do not like to sit at a computer screen and read long instructions or other information. These characteristics of the computer screen medium pose a challenge to the interface designer. The design of every screen should maximize the likelihood that the user's eye will be able to find the important information easily and quickly.

The practices that contribute to this principle are those that

- Use the whole screen rather than putting everything over on the left-hand side.
- Use highlighting techniques to emphasize important information without distracting the user with unnecessary blinking and flashing lights.
- Break up blocks of text by using bulleted lists, numbered steps, and specific examples.
- Put titles on screens and headings on lists.
- Align lists of textual and numeric data to facilitate scanning.

THE GUIDELINES

The next four chapters present the guidelines that contribute to these seven principles. Throughout those chapters I will frequently refer back to these principles to provide a rationale for the importance of a guideline. Each of the guidelines contributes to at least one of the general principles and the general principles together describe the characteristics of an effective user interface.

Chapter 5

Controlling
Transactions

OVERVIEW

Transaction control methods provide the means by which users control the order of screens that are displayed and the options provided by the software. The first guideline describes how to select a transaction control method which is appropriate for your users and the tasks they will perform. The remaining guidelines focus on four transaction control methods: menus, commands, function keys, and question-and-answer dialogue.

- The menu guidelines apply primarily to full screen menus but also apply in some cases to menus that are continually displayed on the top or bottom of a screen or window. The guidelines describe the importance of menu titles, effective menu layout, the ordering and wording of menu options, the methods used to select the options, the appropriate number of options for a menu, and the design of menu hierarchies.
- Function keys can speed up the operation of an application, but the mapping of keys to functions is usually arbitrary. Consequently, users gain speed by having to memorize the key mappings. The number of function keys should be kept to a minimum and you should make sure that they work correctly on all of the equipment on which users might install the software.
- Command names need to be distinct and to clearly describe the functions they perform. You need to provide users with a consistent rule for abbreviating and stacking commands.
- Question and answer dialogue is appropriate only for applications developed for new computer users who are not likely to develop enough experience to be able to deal with the other transaction control methods. The questions in the dialogue are a special case of prompts.

One of the phrases you often read about is the term "menu-driven." It refers to an application program which allows users to control transactions by selecting options from a list. Many people, however, seem to use the term as a synonym for "user-friendly." They seem to believe that the fact that an application has menus and, perhaps, online help makes it effective for the user. As we shall see in this chapter, the presence of menus is no guarantee that the user will not be confused and frustrated. Any transaction control method can be poorly implemented. In fact, poorly designed menus are one of the most common problems with applications software.

This chapter describes guidelines for both the selection and design of the methods by which users control their transactions with a software product. Throughout this chapter I use the term "transaction control" to refer to the means by which the user controls the order and types of screens and operations that an application provides. It is important to keep in mind that controlling the sequence of transactions is not the same as controlling the movement of the cursor on the screen. To make this distinction clear, suppose that a software product allows you to move to a new screen, such as a help screen, by selecting an item from a menu by moving the cursor over the menu options with a mouse and pressing a mouse button to make the choice. The *transaction control* method used in this example is menu selection and the cursor control method is the mouse. Guidelines for controlling the cursor on the screen are contained in Chapter 6 on data entry.

The four transaction control methods we will be discussing are

Menu Selection

Commands

Function Keys

Question-and-Answer Dialogue

Most applications use at least two of these methods; some use more. For you, the interface designer, there are two phases in the design of a transaction control process. First, you must select the transaction control method or methods that are most appropriate for your users, the tasks they will be doing, and the environment in which they will work. Second, the method or methods you choose must be effectively implemented. The next guideline discusses the selection of transaction control methods, while the subsequent guidelines describe their implementation.

SELECTING THE BEST METHOD

Choose the transaction control method that is appropriate for the anticipated level of computer experience of users and for the   performance objectives of the application.(5-1)

The selection of a transaction control method is one of the most important decisions you will make in the design of the software interface, since it determines how and whether the user will be able to control the application. If you select the wrong method, disaster will quickly follow, no matter how well you implement that method. In order to make the right selection, you must have a clear idea about the objectives of the application and a thorough understanding of the level of computer skill of the potential users.

Often the objectives of an application are determined by other people before you begin software development. For example, marketing personnel may have decided that the product must be "menu-driven" or that it must execute quickly to outperform the competition or that it must look like other products your organization has developed. As the designer, you must work within these objectives, which frequently constrain the selection of a method.

There may be, however, additional transaction control decisions to make even when the application's objectives point to one method over the others. For example, if the menus in an application are likely to be too slow for experienced users, you may need to supplement them by allowing users to take shortcuts to speed up operations. In order to make these decisions, you must understand the level of computer skill that the users of the product will have.

I cannot tell you here, in a few words, how to select the right transaction control method for all applications and all types of users. What I can do is to show you that the transaction control methods do differ from each other in several important dimensions and that when you have a choice, these differences should be considered.

There is no transaction control method that is clearly superior to the others for all tasks that both new and experienced computer users will perform. For example, using commands may be effective for experienced users who appreciate their speed, but new users may be confused and frustrated by them. How then do you choose which method to use? The four methods differ on at least two primary dimensions: the cognitive demands that they place on the user and the speed with which they allow transactions to be controlled.

1. Cognitive demands. In general, question and answer dialogue and menus minimize cognitive demands. They do so for two reasons: (1) Users do not have to learn to use any special keys other than the standard keys on the keyboard, and (2) users do not have to recall information from memory because the screens show them the only options available at the time. Commands and function keys do require that the user memorize their functions and later recall them from memory. They also require users to initiate transactions. Users "command" the software by typing commands

or pressing function keys. They have more flexibility in what they can do to control the sequence of events than users of menus or dialogue. Generally, in applications using commands and function keys, nothing happens until the user presses a key or enters a command. But this control puts a cognitive burden on the user to remember the options and how they are used.

2. Speed. The speed with which an application functions is obviously not determined solely by the transaction control method. The efficiency of the software design and the hardware on which it is implemented are the main factors in determining an application's speed. Within the constraints set by the hardware and systems software, however, the transaction control methods do differ in their speed of execution. In general, function keys are the fastest, and question-and-answer dialogue is the slowest. Function keys require only a single keystroke to execute an often complex procedure. On the other hand, question-and-answer dialogue requires the constant passing of control between the user and the application software as each step in the sequence is executed. Commands and menus fall in between these two extremes. While it is often asserted that commands are faster than menus, I do not know of any evidence to support this assertion. But I have seen applications in which commands are faster than menus. Usually, the speed of an application that uses full-screen menus is a function of the time it takes to display the menu screens themselves. Frequently, a well-designed menu structure can be fast enough to satisfy the speed requirements of even experienced users.

When these two dimensions are put together, the four transaction control methods can be roughly ordered according to their appropriateness for the level of computer experience of potential users. The following list of methods is ordered by the demands they place on the user, from the fewest to the most:

Question-and-answer Dialogue
Menus
Function Keys
Commands

Sequences of question-and-answer dialogue are appropriate only for applications developed for users who have little or no computer experience and who are not likely to develop enough experience to be able to deal with the other methods. Some educational and training applications will fit into this category. For most applications that will be operated by new and moderately skilled users, menus are an appropriate choice. The extensive use of function keys and commands is appropriate for users who have a good deal of computer experience and who will be using the application frequently.

While you can use this order as a rough guide to the selection of a transaction control method, it does not apply to a case you will frequently encounter, namely an application that is intended for both the new and experienced user. A new word processing program may be a good example. If your organization developed such a program, it would probably want to sell it to both new and experienced users and would also expect that new users would eventually become experienced ones. Furthermore, since editing speed would likely be a critical selling point to potential customers, the fastest transaction control methods would be considered. One solution to these requirements that has often been taken is to make use of function keys and commands but to supplement the applications software with online help, tutorials, exercises, and even training courses.

There are other types of applications where the solution to meeting the requirements of a variety of skill levels is not as clear. For example, a typical electronic mail system will be used by many new and casual users as well as a few experienced, frequent users. One good solution to this problem is to provide users with two methods of transaction control, such as menus and commands. Users are then allowed to choose between the two methods. For example, in an electronic mail system that I have encountered, users are allowed to switch back and forth between the two methods by typing either a Ctrl-C for "command mode" or Ctrl-M for "menu mode." In this case, the control mode is faster than the menu mode but does put a burden on the user's memory to remember the commands.

There is a technique that can be used to meet the requirements of both new and experienced users. It does not provide a clear separation between commands and menus, but it does speed up the operation of the application. To use this technique, you must design your menus so that the menu options are selected by typing a letter sequence, such as DEL for an option to delete a record. Users are then allowed to type more than one letter sequence at a time on a menu to move directly to where they want to go. To illustrate this technique, Exhibit 5-1 shows a menu screen in which the user has typed EM R. This sequence allows users to see a display of their first mail message immediately. New users would type EM here and then a second menu would be displayed from which they would

Exhibit 5-1 Example of a menu that allows the user to stack options.

Office Management

```
Options:


EM   Electronic Mail
PH   PHone Directory
MM   Meeting Management
WP   Word Processing


H    Help
Q    Quit
```

```
Type your choice:EM R
```

---

select R to read their first mail message. Thus the experienced users gain speed by knowing that they can stack the commands together.

Up to this point, we have been discussing the skill and experience of the user. But do not ignore the level of skill it takes to design these methods effectively. If you have ever designed a large application that makes use of commands and function keys, you know how difficult it is to do well. As we will see in the next section, designing menus is not as easy as it appears, but, in my opinion, it is still easier than designing a command language. My advice to any software designer who does not have the experience, time, and resources to design and test a complex application that uses commands and function keys is to keep the transaction control method simple. Generally, menus will be the safest choice. Remember the principle we discussed in the last chapter, that you usually should favor the new user in your design. The selection of a transaction control method is a case where this principle can be applied. Ideally, of course, the needs of all users should be met. But when the budget and/or the software engineering resources are limited, simplicity is essential. It is better, in my opinion, to have a few skilled users who wish the application were faster than to have a large number of casual users who are frustrated and confused.

Whichever transaction control method you choose, subject it to extensive testing with a sample of potential users, revise it when it needs improvement, and test it again.

MENUS

Menus have become, perhaps, the most frequently used method of transaction control.   They are usually the preferred method of transaction control for software that is intended for new or casual users.   Despite their widespread use, however, menus are a relatively new feature of applications software.   A comprehensive summary of user-interface guidelines published about ten years ago (Engel and Granda 1975) does not include guidelines for menus, which were not then in common use.

For new or casual users, menus have two major advantages over other transaction control methods.   First, they provide an obvious structure to the software.   In a well-designed interface that is controlled by menus, the user can quickly develop an understanding of how the software is structured from the organization of the options on menus and from the organization of the menus themselves.   The ability of new users to form an accurate mental model of the structure of the software is a major contributor to their feeling about being in control (Norman 1983).   See Guideline 8-25 for a more detailed explanation of this concept.   Second, menus take advantage of people's superior ability to recognize information rather than to recall it from memory (McNulty 1965).

Menus also have advantages for you as the designer.   The availability of software development tools, such as forms managers, has made it easy to create menus from design specifications.   As you will see, however, the design of an effective menu can still be difficult even with these tools.   While an effective menu looks simple, its design requires careful thought.   The guidelines in this section describe how to create better menus.

Types of Menus

The example menus shown in Exhibits 5-2 and 5-3 are typical full-screen menus.   They consist of a vertical list of options displayed on a screen or in a window on a screen without other parts of the application being displayed on the screen or window with them. When the user selects an option, the menu is erased and a new display appears.   The full-screen menu is the most frequently used menu type.

However, other types of menus have begun to appear more frequently.   There are at least three types of menus, in addition to the full-screen menu, that are now in common use: a list of single word options displayed horizontally below or, less frequently, above an application area of the screen (See Exhibit 5-4.); a strip menu,

Exhibit 5-2   Example of a Poorly Designed Menu

```
***Menu

01   ADD PROJECT INFO
02   FILE DELETION
03   UPDATE PROJECT INFO
04   DISPLAY PROJECT INFO
05   REPORT MODIFICATION
06   REPORT OUTPUT
07   QUIT

ENTER OPTION:06
```

which is a horizontal list of pictures (icons) that represent the menu options and that are also displayed above or below an application area; and a pop-up menu, which is displayed beside, or in some cases, over an application. Unlike full-screen menus, each of the other menu types is displayed on the screen while some portion of the application is also displayed. Some horizontal word and strip menus also remain on the screen throughout an application. Pop-up menus are usually requested with a mouse button and disappear when the user makes a choice.

The menu guidelines described below focus on the design of full screen menus because they are the most frequently used menu type. Where appropriate, however, the guidelines are applied to the other menu types.

Exhibit 5-2 contains an example of a poorly designed, full-screen menu. Exhibit 5-3 shows an improved version of the same

Exhibit 5-3   An Improved Menu

```
                    Manage Project Descriptions

          Options:

                    1. Add a project.
                    2  Update a project.
                    3. Display a project.
                    4. Delete a project.

                    5. Print/Display project reports.
                    6. Update project reports.

                    7. Return to previous menu.

          Type option number:_
```

menu that is consistent with the guidelines described in this section. I will use these examples throughout this section to help you to understand the meaning of the guidelines.

Put a meaningful title on the top of every menu.(5-2)

This guideline applies primarily to full-screen menus. Strip and horizontal menus that remain on the screen throughout an application can be used without a title. Note that the title on the menu shown in Exhibit 5-2 is not very informative. As the title suggests, it certainly is a menu, but so is every menu. The title does not say what the menu contains or give any indication about how the menu fits into the sequence or hierarchy of menus in the application. The example menu in Exhibit 5-3 has an improved title that describes the menu's contents. The words in the title have been more carefully chosen. They provide a name that categorizes the options in the menu in a meaningful way.

Exhibit 5-4 A horizontal single-word menu

—

Advanced Copy Format Load Quit Search

A menu title may also describe the level of the menu in a menu hierarchy. For example, a title such as "Main Electronic Mail Menu" describes both the level of the menu and its contents. However, avoid the tendency to substitute a level description, such as "Main Menu," for a title. When the title contains information about the level of the menu, it should also describe the options.

For full-screen menus, provide symmetric balance by centering the title and the menu options around the center axis of the screen.(5-3)

The example in Exhibit 5-3 shows a menu that is pushed over to the left-hand side of the screen. This is typically done for the convenience of the programmer. It provides no advantage to the user, however, and confines all of the text to one area of the screen. See guideline 6-4 for further discussion of the use of symmetric balance.

Choose an organizing principle for the menu options.(5-4)

As you can see, there does not appear to be any recognizable order to the menu options displayed in Exhibit 5-2. The DELETE option has been placed second but it is not likely to be the second most frequently used option nor is it the second operation in the normal sequence of events. The menu options shown in Exhibit 5-3 have been partitioned into groups and then reordered by their logical sequence of operations, that is, by the order of tasks that users will use to accomplish their work. For example, users will first add a project description, modify it, review it, and, occasionally, delete it.

For full screen menus, there are three commonly used organizing principles:

- Expected frequency of use
- Logical sequence of operations
- Alphabetical order

In most cases, you can order the options by either their logical sequence or their frequency. When you can't use either of these because there is no obvious logical order and you cannot predict the frequency of use, then use alphabetical order. It at least provides an ordering method with which the user is familiar. Alphabetical ordering may also be effective when there are a large number of menu options, such as more than about eight. As the number of options grows, users must spend more time scanning the options to find the one they want. Alphabetical ordering provides an easy means to facilitate this scanning. If the menu contains options from more than one category, such as the edit options and the report options shown in Exhibit 5-3, group the options in each category together and then choose an organizing principle for each category.

Word menus that are displayed horizontally should be in alphabetical order unless the number of choices is very small, such as five or less. It is much harder to scan a horizontal menu because the first letters of the options do not all start in the same column.

In this instance, alphabetical ordering is the only ordering method recommended because users are sufficiently familiar with it to enable them to locate options with this type of menu.

You obviously cannot order strip menus with icons alphabetically. But, you can still use either of the other two ordering methods.

To facilitate scanning, put blank lines between logical groupings of menu options and after about every fifth option in a long list.(5-5)

The options shown in Exhibit 5-2 look like they all belong to the same category. The extra blank lines shown in Exhibit 5-3, however, make it clear that there are actually three categories of options here. They also make it easier to find the options within a category.

Limit the number of menu choices to one screen.(5-6)

I don't know of any magic number that limits the number of options in a menu, except that they all should fit on one screen. There is a lively debate in the human factors literature, however, around the issue of determining the optimum size of a menu (Paap and Roske-Hofstrand 1986; MacGregor and Newman 1986). The current research seems to indicate that the optimum number of items per screen depends on the complexity of the options and how they are organized. When the options are simple, such as a list of single words, and are effectively organized into groups, the optimum number of options can be quite high, the investigated range being 16 to 78. When the options require the user to read a phrase or sentence, however, the optimum number is closer to five items. In fact, several recent studies have shown that when all other factors are equal, it is better to have a few longer menus, such as about eight items, than many small ones, such as two to four items (Snowberry and others 1983; Kiger 1984; Parkinson and others 1985). More research is needed, however, to further clarify this issue. As a rule of thumb, organize a menu hierarchy according to the tasks users will perform (See Guideline 5-14.), and organize the options on each screen in a way to minimize the users search time. (See Guideline 5-4.) If your menu options consist of more than single words, limit the number of options to about 5-8. If a menu contains more than 8-10 options, there is probably more than one category of information contained in it. In such a case, consider breaking up the menu into two or more menus, each with a more homogeneous category of options.

Use an option selection method that is consistent with the technology available at the user's work station and the size of the application being designed. (5-7)

Choosing a method by which the user selects an option from a menu involves a set of trade-offs that are determined by a number of factors, such as (1) the technology available at the user's work station and (2) the size of your application.   The three most frequently available technologies are the traditional keyboard, the touch screen, and the mouse. If the work station for which you are designing software has a touch screen or a mouse, then these devices should be used for option selection. With the touch screen, users simply touch the option with their finger.   With a mouse, users move the cursor over the menu with the mouse and select an option by clicking a mouse button. Both of these methods are quick and straightforward.

More difficult trade-offs occur with full-screen menus which must be displayed on work stations that only have a keyboard. There are usually three competing alternatives:

- Select by number
- Select by letter or letter combination
- Select by cursor movement

There is some disagreement about which of these methods is the best (Brown and others (1981); Pew and Rollins (1975)). Let's examine the advantages and disadvantages of these methods.

Letters have three advantages over numbers.   First, they provide a meaningful mapping between the value of the choice and its function. For example, the letters DEL can be typed to select the option to DELETE a record. Second, letters make it easy to add or delete options to the menu without changing the order of the other options.   With numbers, any change in an option requires the renumbering of the other options. Third, letters make it relatively easy to stack options together. As the example in Exhibit 5-1 shows, the user can move directly to read an electronic mail message by typing EM for Electronic Mail and R for Read on the same menu instead of typing EM on the first menu and then R on the second. This feature allows experienced users to move quickly through a series of menus with one command string. The arbitrary mapping of numbers to options makes stacking difficult when numbers are used to select options.

However, numbers also can have advantages over letters; they are simpler for you to create and they are not likely to confuse the user. As the size of a program grows, it becomes harder to find unique letter combinations that are not easily confused with each other. With very small applications, single letters can be used to select options. For example, D can be typed for an option to DELETE a file. As the number of options grows, however, you are forced to use a longer sequence, such as DEL for DELETE to distinguish it from such options as DEF for DEFER or DIS for DISPLAY. The user is more likely to confuse these similar letter combinations, resulting in errors. As the number of options grows, you will find it difficult to design menu options that are unique but distinct from one another.

These differences between numbers and letter combinations as option selection methods indicate that the advantages that letter combinations provide can be achieved only at the cost of more extensive design and testing. If the application is large, such as more than ten menus, it is normally easier and less risky to use numbers to select menu options.

Selection by cursor movement is the slowest of the selection methods. This method is usually implemented by allowing users to move the cursor or a highlighted area to the desired option with an arrow key or the spacebar and then pressing the RETURN or ENTER key to select it. Except for certain educational and training applications, this method is usually too slow for even moderately skilled users. You can overcome this disadvantage by allowing the user to select an option by using either of two methods: moving the cursor to the option or entering the first letter of the option.

Provide a way for the user to leave the menu without choosing an option.(5-8)

Frequently, the user gets to a menu by mistake or decides after displaying a menu to perform some procedure that is located on another menu. Consequently, every menu screen should provide the user with a means to leave the screen without choosing one of the other menu options. There are several ways to implement this procedure. For example, you can assign a function key which takes the user to some other place in the application, usually a main menu, or you can put an option on each menu, such as "Return to previous screen." If you use a function key, you may also want to put a status message, such as "F1=Budget Menu," on the screen to tell the user that the option is available. See Guideline 8-7 for a more detailed explanation of these messages. Frequently, you may want to give the user more than one exit option on a menu, such as one to go to another menu or screen and one to leave the application completely.

Use words for your menu options that clearly and specifically describe what the user is selecting; use simple, active verbs to describe menu options.(5-9)

I have already addressed the need to provide a specific and meaningful title for each menu. The wording of the menu options and the prompt at the bottom of the screen asking the user to type an option are equally important, however. As a design team develops a software product over a number of months or years, they gradually begin to use a set of words and phrases among themselves to describe the components of the product. These words often reflect the unique or special capabilities of the components. The design team often feels a sense of pride about these special features they are creating and, therefore, they feel the need to use special words to describe them. These special words frequently appear in menu options. Unfortunately, users have not been through the development process and may not have used competing products. They will only be confused by words that are not simple, direct, and straightforward, I will have more to say about using plain English in Chapter 8. Here we will apply the guidelines described there to the special case of menus.

As you can see, the wording of the choices shown in Exhibit 5-2 is less than informative.

1. What is PROJECT INFO? This description needs to be more specific. Furthermore, there in no reason to abbreviate any of the words on this menu. In the example shown in Exhibit 5-3, the options have been described in more specific language and all the words have been spelled out.

2. Is the term "FILE" in the second option in Exhibit 5-2 meant to be a synonym for the term "PROJECT INFO"? Here is an example of the use of computer jargon that the programmer understands but that is likely to confuse the user.

3. What is the difference between "UPDATE" and "MODIFICATION" in the menu shown in Exhibit 5-2? Do these words denote different operations or are the two different words used to denote the same operation? The example in Exhibit 5-3 shows that the words used in Exhibit 5-2 have the same meaning. Consequently, the word "Update" has been used in both cases.

4. Some of the options contain active verbs, such as "ADD," while others do not. Words such as "DELETION," "MODIFICATION," and "OUTPUT" are attempts to use nouns as verbs.

5. What does "QUIT" mean on this menu? Some obvious possibilities are (1) to leave the application program and be logged out; (2) to leave the program and not be logged out; or (3) to return to the main menu or to some other menu. Exhibit 5-3 shows that when users select this quit option, they will be returned to the previous screen. Consequently, this option says specifically what its selection will accomplish.

6. Finally, the prompt below the menu instructs the user to ENTER an option. "Enter" is a vague term that is being used here to mean "Type your option and then press the ENTER key." In Exhibit 5-3 the word "ENTER" has been replaced by the word "Type."

In general, the selection of words for a menu screen should follow these rules:

- Use words that clearly describe the options.
- Use common English words rather than computer or other jargon. Spell out the words completely.
- Use simple, active verbs to tell users what actions will result from their choice. Users are selecting from a menu because they want to do something. In English, only verbs can be used to describe actions. I prefer to start each option with the verb. Do not try to use nouns as verbs. They are not only awkward, but also are frequently ambiguous. They can also make your menus appear formal and abstract. See Chapter 8 for a more complete discussion of the use of plain English.
- Be sure that the option to leave the menu describes the consequences of its selection completely. Reserve words such as "Quit" for cases in which the user will be transferred completely out of the application.
- Describe the options with parallel construction. For example, if single words are used for the options, use the same part of speech for all the options. Action verbs are preferable.
- The prompt below the menu should instruct the user to "Type" a number or letter(s) or to "Press" a function key, rather than the vague "Enter" or the frequently misused "Hit."

You will find that choosing the words for a menu will be easier if you have a glossary of terms in your user-interface handbook. (See

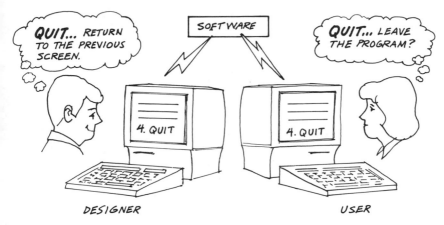

Figure 5-1   Exit menu options should specifically describe their effect

Chapter 3.) The glossary ensures consistency within an application, when there is a team of people developing it, and also across applications.

Use icons that unambiguously identify the meaning of the user's options.(5-10)

The phrase "a picture is worth a thousand words" has often been quoted to emphasize the advantages of pictures.   There is ample evidence that human beings process pictorial information in a different way than from words (Lodding 1983). We have the ability to extract complex concepts from simple pictures in a instant. Some interface designs have taken advantage of this ability by presenting the options available to the user as pictures, called icons, rather than describing them in words. Some of these designs have been very successful. However, select icons with care. It can be difficult to create icons that are effective. The meaning of pictures can be infinitely more ambiguous than the meaning of words. It is easy to identify a picture of a wastebasket on a video screen. But how does it function? If I put an old document into it, is it gone? Can I empty the wastebasket as well as fill it? Do I have more space available after I put a document in the wastebasket or do I have to empty it first? The icon tells us a lot, but it also leaves a lot unsaid.

The developers of some of the early systems using icons spent a substantial amount of time testing human subjects to find an effective set of icons (Smith 1982). You should be prepared to conduct such tests if you intend to use icons. It is the only way to be sure that they are unambiguous and convey the exact meaning you intend.

Minimize the highlighting used on a menu.(5-11)

Highlighting refers to the display of information in special formats to emphasize its importance. For example, colors, reverse video, or intensity differences are often used to emphasize information. The use of highlighting is discussed in detail in Chapter 6. Guideline 6-20 in that chapter makes the point that the overuse of highlighting is one of the most frequently abused practices in interface design and makes it more difficult for the user to recognize important information when it is being displayed. The example menu shown in Exhibit 5-2 has three instances of highlighting that are not needed: (1) the asterisks before the title; (2) the added brightness of the option selection numbers; and (3) the added brightness of the prompt at the bottom of the menu. Since the prompt and a title occur on all menus, there is no need to highlight them. They are not important or critical information. The main body of a menu, which contains the menu options, does not ordinarily require any highlighting. The only situation where you may need highlighting is when there is some exception to normal practice that the user should be made aware of.

Do not require the user to enter leading or trailing blanks or zeros, and do not include a default value on a menu.(5-12)

Exhibit 5-2 shows a menu that forces the user to enter the leading zero for every menu choice. This practice violates one of the rules of data entry: the user should never be required to enter leading or trailing blanks, zeros, or other characters. (See Guideline 7-8.) This type of requirement usually occurs because a programmer has written the code so that it will read only a two-digit number that is right justified. This is a needless restriction that users will not know about until they make an error or receive an error message and reenter the number in the only format that will be accepted. This sequence wastes time and leads to frustration for the user. Do not require the user to enter these values.

The use of a default value on a menu will also cause errors. A default is a menu choice that is automatically selected when the user presses the return key without typing a choice. You might consider using a default to speed menu selection for a frequently used option. The first time the computer responds slowly or users are distracted for a moment, however, they are likely to press the RETURN key to see if the program is still executing. When this happens on a menu with a default value, users will be transferred to some other part of the software or may even be logged off by the computer. This is likely to make users confused and angry. Do not use default values on menus.

Display the menu options in mixed, upper and lower case letters. (5-13)

The menu options shown in Exhibit 5-2 are all displayed in upper case. As a general rule, the only time that text should be displayed in upper case is when it is done for special emphasis. Otherwise, all text should be in mixed, upper and lower case format. See Guideline 6-8 for the rationale behind this general rule.

Organize menu hierarchies according to the tasks users will perform, rather than the structure of the software modules.(5-14)

One of the major advantages of menus is that they provide structure to an application. Users can look at the menus and the menu options to help them form a mental model of how the application is organized. The organization you build into your menu hierarchy, however, can either help users to quickly build an accurate model of the structure or it can confuse them.

The organization that makes the most sense to users is the one that maps the way they accomplish their work. The main menu of the application should partition the components into units that reflect the functions or tasks that users will perform with the software. To design this and other menus effectively, you or someone on your design team must understand how your users think about and accomplish their work. Ideally, you should have a user representative on your team. When this is not possible, you must have someone available who can provide a task analysis of the users' job.

The problem of designing an effective menu hierarchy is especially difficult when the application you are developing does not simply automate some manual task but provides users with new capabilities they did not have before. In that case, you cannot

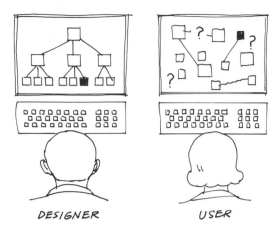

Figure 5-2 Design the menu hierarchy around user's tasks

simply analyze what people are doing now, you have to imagine how they will use the new capabilities. I urge you to conduct usability tests on your menus as early in the design process as possible. The prototyping tools now available make it possible to create a prototype of a menu hierarchy in a matter of hours or, at most, a few days. With these tools, you can create a menu hierarchy before or during the development of the software. Prototyping will give you the flexibility to make a reasonable guess about the design of the hierarchy and allow you to test it.

The most frequent mistake that designers make in creating a menu hierarchy is to organize it according to the hierarchy of the software modules that are used to structure the design of the application. Modern, top-down, structured design techniques require that you break up your main module into a set of subordinate modules and then in turn break these up into smaller units. It seems only natural, therefore, to make the menus map this structure. However, the organization of the software modules that is most effective to the software engineer is not necessarily the one that is the most effective to users. The structure of the menu hierarchy does not have to map the structure of the software hierarchy. Once you understand this point, you are free from a constraining influence that can force you to design a menu hierarchy that does not relate to the tasks users will perform with the application.

FUNCTION KEYS

Most modern computer terminals and microcomputers contain three groups of keys on their keyboards. (1) The largest group, usually positioned on the left-hand side of the keyboard, contains a standard QWERTY keyboard and some additional keys such as those labeled "DEL" and "BACKSPACE." These keys are used to type the letters of the alphabet and numbers and to perform some special functions such as deleting the previous character typed. (2) On the right-hand side of the keyboard, there is usually a numeric key pad that contains, in matrix format, the numbers 0 to 9 and several additional keys such as those labeled "+," "-," and "=." These keys are usually used to enter numeric values in applications that require extensive data entry. (3) Above or to one side of these two key pads are usually one or more rows of keys labeled "F1," "F2," etc. These keys are referred to as function keys or, in some cases programmable function keys, because they do not have a function until you assign it. For example, the F2 key has no function until you decide that it will be used to display a help message on the screen.

These three keyboard areas may appear to serve three different functions. On closer examination, however, the distinctions between them are not so clear. In fact, the function of any key can be changed by the software. For example, the BACKSPACE key is often assigned by the software to function as a backtab key which allows the user to move backwards through the fields of a data entry screen. The only difference between the function keys and the other keys is that the function keys do not have a meaning outside of the the one you give them in an application. But you can change the function of any key.

The term "function key," as it is used here, refers to the assignment of any key, by application software, to perform a function other than its normal one. Thus, the F2 key that is used to display help and the BACKSPACE key that is used as a backtab are both function keys in this sense.

Use function keys sparingly to speed up the execution of frequently used operations.(5-15)

For a user, function keys are a mixed blessing. On the one hand, they do speed up frequently used procedures. The mapping of function keys to the operations they perform, however, is always arbitrary and is almost always different from application to application. This requires the user to learn this mapping and to remember it. For applications that require extensive data entry or data base manipulations, function keys normally cannot be avoided. For those applications, you should provide online help that shows the mapping of the keys to their function. (See Guideline 8-24.)

For small applications that you expect will be used by a wide variety of new and casual users, my advice is to avoid using keys that are not on the standard QWERTY keyboard. When you do, you impose a cognitive burden on the user that is not normally offset by the improved speed they provide. Function keys can also cause the problems described in the next guideline.

Be sure that any function keys that you use will operate correctly on all of the keyboards users have.(5-16)

There are no standards that regulate the bit pattern that a keyboard generates when a key other than a normal QWERTY key and a few others is pressed. Therefore, whenever a function key or a key on the numeric key pad is used by an application, there is no guarantee that a different terminal will have the same key on it. If your users have more than one type of terminal or if there are several different types of microcomputers they use, you should make sure that any key that you use in the software works on all of the equipment.

In an organization with which I once worked, there were two different terminals in use when we were developing a major new software product. The first terminal had four function keys on the top row of the numeric key pad. The second had sixteen function keys above the QWERTY key pad. Of the sixteen, the first four transmitted the same bit pattern as the four function keys on the first terminal. We decided to use only these four function keys in the software and to modify our documentation to explain where these keys were located. We felt satisfied with this solution until just before the product was to become operational. An outside event beyond our control complicated our solution. Another division of the organization decided to buy a large number of new microcomputers. Unfortunately, the function keys on the microcomputer were different from the keys on either of the other terminals. The mapping of the four function keys that we had selected for our application onto the microcomputer keyboard was worse than if we had selected them at random. Our ultimate solution to this problem was to purchase a software tool that made the microcomputer emulate one of our other terminals. In the meantime, some of our users were prevented from using the application. If we had known in advance about the new microcomputers, we would have considered not using any function keys.

This example illustrates the possibility that using function keys can lock out or confuse many of your users. Check out this possibility before you select a function key and then hope that new equipment doesn't undo your plans. Better yet, if you can, avoid this problem by using only the keys on the main QWERTY keyboard to perform all of the functions needed for your application.

COMMANDS

A command language is a set of commands that allows users to control their transactions with an application by typing a word or an abbreviation of a word to indicate what it is they wish the software to do. Before the widespread use of menus, commands were the primary method of transaction control. Commands are still in common use and are likely to remain so. The following guidelines describe the rules for designing commands.

Use common, short English words that clearly describe the action that the command will carry out; choose words that are distinctive from one another.(5-17)

The objective of a command language is to allow users to "command" the software to execute their wishes by typing a short word or an abbreviation for a word. Ideally, the words should be short English verbs that are clear and unambiguous in their meaning to the user. For example, it is not a good practice to make the user type REPRODUCE or MULTIPLY when COPY would do. As the number of commands increases, however, the likelihood that any two commands will be confused grows. Furthermore, the distinctiveness of commands applies not only to the verbs themselves but also to their abbreviations. (See the next guideline.)

It is not a simple job to design command names that are simple and clear to the user and that will not be confused. If you have ever used an extensive command language, you know that some very strange names are often needed to avoid confusion. To avoid this ambiguity and confusion, look carefully at other command languages to see how other people have solved this problem. Then create a glossary of commands that your team members can use, and test your commands with potential users. For any commands that give users problems, modify these commands and then retest them.

Allow the user to shorten commands by using a consistent rule for abbreviating them.(5-18)

As I stated earlier in this chapter, the major advantage of commands is that they provide a potential speed and flexibility advantage over other transaction control methods. Command languages, however, do require users to type letter combinations, which is a very error prone activity. One way you can minimize typing errors and speed up transactions with the software is to allow experienced users to type a shortened version of the command. It seems only logical that if you have decided to use commands because they are fast, then you must also allow users to shorten them. Unfortunately, shortening commands increases the likelihood that users will be confused and that errors will be made. Some of this confusion can be eliminated by having a consistent rule for shortening them. The research in this area suggests that simple truncation is the best rule to use (Ehrenreich and Porcu 1982). For example, allowing the user to type the first three letters of a command is a simple rule that users can easily understand when it is used consistently.

Many applications that I have used take a "let the user beware" attitude toward truncation. What I mean here is that the designer has allowed the user to type any unique letter combination as a command. For example, if I type DEL for DELETE and there are no other commands that begin with DEL, then the software will execute the command. I might even be able to get away with just DE here. The only way to know is to try it and that is where the problem lies. I once lost an hour's work to an application that allowed me to play this truncation game. It was an electronic mail system that made it possible to defer the sending of a mail message to a later day and time. For example, I could defer sending a message to my boss until next Monday morning. The menu screen that contained the defer option displayed DEF as the command to use. I knew from experience, however, that the software allowed me to truncate commands further when they are unique. In this case I tried DE. Unfortunately, the software interpreted DE as a truncation for DELETE but not for DEFER. In addition, the software did not have a verification prompt that asked me if I really wanted to delete the message. Consequently, I lost the message I had created. This example shows you several features that are as poorly designed as the truncation rule. The point here, however, is that it is better to have a consistent rule for shortening commands than to make the user guess at which letter combinations will work.

Allow the user to stack a series of commands on one line.(5-19)

Unless you allow the user to issue more than one command at a time, commands have a less significant time advantage over menus. The time it takes to display a full screen menu may be greater than the time to display a prompt for a command. This advantage, however, is offset by the increased likelihood that the user will mistype the command and have to enter it two or more times. By typing a string of commands at one time, the user can execute several procedures at once. This activity will increase the speed of transactions.

However, this feature can lead to confusion when the user makes an error. Typically, your software will read the command string and execute it one command at a time. If users make a mistake in the third command, they may not be sure if the first two have been executed. You should clear up this ambiguity by providing the user with feedback as each command is executed. When it is not obvious by the actions on the screen that a command has been successfully completed, display a status message that tells the user what is happening. Guidelines 8-7, 8-8, and 8-9 show you how to design these messages. In addition, when users make a mistake, display a clear and specific error message that tells them which command is in error and what to do about it. (See Guideline 8-12.)

Allow the user to display a list of commands.(5-20)

Providing a list of legal commands is a form of help that is absolutely essential when commands are being used for transaction control. The user should be able to display the list by using a function key or by typing a help option. The commands should be listed alphabetically. It would also help to provide a short phrase beside each command that describes its function or allows users to get further help on each command. Be sure, however, to design the help you provide on commands according to the guidelines in Chapter 8.

QUESTION-AND-ANSWER DIALOGUE

The questions in a question-and-answer dialogue are examples of prompts. Since the guidelines for prompts are described in Chapter 8, I will not repeat them here. (See especially Guidelines 8-8, 8-9, and 8-10.)

TRANSACTION CONTROL CONSISTENCY

The final guideline in this chapter is similar to the guidelines on consistency which end each of the subsequent chapters.

Be consistent in the use of menu formats, procedures, and wording; the mapping of keys to functions; the naming and abbreviation of commands; and the design of question-and-answer prompts.(5-21)

One of the most important characteristics of an effective user interface is the consistent way that it displays information to the user and responds to the the user's input. This consistency makes it possible for the user to carry over habits learned from one part of the interface to others. As in all of the components of interface design described in this book, consistency in transaction control is essential. But consistency can be achieved only when all of the members of your team agree to follow the same conventions and you communicate these conventions to them in a document such as a user-interface handbook. (See Chapter 3.)

Chapter 6

Displaying
Information

OVERVIEW

Where information is placed on the screen and the form in which it is displayed are critical to the productivity of users. Layout and format are not just cosmetic factors. They should help users to find what they are looking for and to read or scan it easily. This chapter first describes seven general guidelines which apply to all types of displays, including putting a title on every screen, displaying information in a form that does not require users to translate it to understand it, using the whole screen rather than just the left-hand side, and selecting a windowing system that is consistent with the users' experience and the tasks they will perform.

The eighteen specific guidelines cover three broad areas: text, tables and lists, and the highlighting of important information.

- Text should be displayed in mixed, upper and lower case rather than in all upper case, have a ragged right margin, and avoid hyphenation, unnecessary abbreviations, and acronyms.

- Tables and lists should help users find the information they need. Columns and rows need meaningful labels and the order of items should facilitate scanning. Alphabetic data is left justified while numeric data is right justified or aligned by decimal points or other delimiters. Extra spaces between columns and rows of long lists will facilitate legibility.

- Highlighting helps users to see important information and to avoid becoming distracted. Select highlighting methods that are appropriate for the level of importance of the information being highlighted. Strong techniques such as blinking and audible tones should be reserved for critical information. Color, used to highlight, should be compatible with the human visual system and color combinations should complement each other.

The video display has revolutionized our communications with computers. In the mid 1970s, I used my first terminal with a video screen. At the time, I wasn't sure I liked it. While it was much more attractive than terminals using a roll of paper, I couldn't see any great advantage to the screen. I had trouble feeling comfortable with the concept of a cursor and how to move it. I was also confused by scrolling, because my mental model of a video terminal was that it was a substitute for a piece of paper. It took me a while to see it as a window through which I could view moving information.

Back then it never occurred to me that communicating with software by typing on a roll of paper, which is how I saw the interaction occurring, could, in any way, limit the communication process. I typed my commands or data on the paper and the software typed its response. By current standards, these transactions were slow, but they didn't seem so then.

Now I cannot imagine being without a video display. It has so many great advantages. For example, I do not believe that menus would have ever become the common method of controlling transactions without the video terminal. Waiting for the options to be typed on paper would have been too slow. As with communicating on paper, however, the video terminal is a medium which has its limitations. I will be describing its limitations as well as its strengths throughout the next three chapters.

It is important for you, as an interface designer, to appreciate that where you place information on the screen and the form in which you display it are critical to the productivity of users. Layout and form are not cosmetic issues. We will not be talking in this chapter about making displays pretty, but how to make them effective. In this context, "effective" means that (1) the layout of the screen helps users to find what they are looking for and (2) the form in which information is displayed helps them to read or scan it.

Unfortunately, the effective layout of information is not a skill in which most computer professionals have any training. Most programmers, software engineers, and even human factors specialists are not taught the principles of the layout and format of information. Programmers may be shown how to format program code so that a maintenance programmer can more easily read it, but their training usually does not include how to display information for users. The objective of this chapter is to make you aware of layout and format issues and to provide guidelines to make your displays more effective.

The chapter begins with some general display guidelines, continues with guidelines for displaying text, tables, and lists, and concludes with guidelines for highlighting important information.

GENERAL DISPLAY GUIDELINES

The guidelines in this section apply to all types of displays, whether they contain menus, text, lists of information, or a combination of all three. Rather than repeating these guidelines throughout this and the other chapters, they are grouped together here.

Put a title on every display screen that clearly and specifically describes the contents of the screen.(6-1)

It is absolutely essential that you put a meaningful title at the top of every data display, menu, help, and data entry screen. Titles have an important function. Numerous research studies have shown that organizing features, such as titles, increase the comprehension and retention of information (Ausubel 1978; Dooling and Mullet 1973). They act as organizers around which users store and retrieve information from memory.

It is even more critical to use titles on screens than on a page in paper documents. Remember that in a paper document you can easily flip back a page or a chapter, or even go back to the table of contents, to help put information in context. A video screen makes this process cumbersome, even when it is possible. Users should not have to move from the screen they are on to another screen to interpret what they see on the screen. It is critical that you always make what is being displayed clear to users and, if appropriate, identify the screen location in the application.

The wording of the title should tell the user what is being displayed. Avoid using vague terms such as "data" or "information." On menu screens avoid the temptation to label the first menu in an application the "Main Menu." (See Guideline 5-2.) Put some qualifier on the title, such as "Financial Planning Main Menu." This title not only describes the level of the menu but also its contents.

Display only information that the user needs to know.(6-2)

Until recently, I was reluctant to propose this guideline because it seems so obvious that no one would violate it. Who would bother to include information on a screen that the user does not need? However, as I spend more time evaluating software, I continue to find examples, such as the menu shown in Exhibit 6-1, that violate this guideline. There is no reason for the user to have to see all of the empty options in this menu. It is not only unnecessary, but it also distracts the user by bringing to mind all sorts of questions. For example, why are there fourteen options here? What will eventually go into these empty options? Don't distract users by displaying information that they do not need to know.

Don't make the user translate displayed data into other units or to refer to documentation to interpret the meaning of what is

Exhibit 6-1   A Menu Containing Information the User Does Not Need

```
                        MAIN MENU

1.  Mail                      8.  Left blank for later use
2.  Scheduling                9.  Left blank for later use
3.  Reports                  10.  Left blank for later use
4.  Left blank for later use 11.  Left blank for later use
5.  Left blank for later use 12.  Left blank for later use
6.  Left blank for later use 13.  Left blank for later use
7.  Left blank for later use 14.  QUIT

                    Enter option:
```

Display data to the user in directly usable form.(6-3)

displayed on the screen. One of my earliest recollections of using a mainframe computer is my struggle with translating octal numbers to decimal. The machine I was using displayed the number of bytes of memory that I was allowed to use in octal format. Requesting an additional 1000 bytes meant adding 1750 to my previous total. There was no need for me, the user, to have to make this conversion.

Error message numbers are another example of a violation of this guideline. The user should not have to go to a book to look up an error number to find out what went wrong. (See Guideline 8-9.)

Provide symmetric balance to displays by centering titles and headings and by placing information on both sides of the center axis.(6-4)

Throughout this book, there are numerous examples of poor user-interface practices. (See Exhibits 5-2 and 7-2.) Among their other problems, most of these examples show displays in which the text is pushed over to the left-hand side of the screen. Perhaps programmers do this because it is easier for them to create the display; perhaps they believe that since people read from the left that it is somehow faster for people if the information begins on the left-hand side. The fact that figures and illustrations in paper documents are displayed symmetrically should tell you that this is not true. When you restrict your displays to the left-hand side of the screen, you do not leave yourself room to format information in ways that emphasize what is important to the user. Menus, lists, data entry forms, and online documentation should all be symmetrical on the screen, and titles and headings should be centered.

Every display should indicate how to exit from the screen.(6-5)

Never put users into a situation of not knowing how to exit from the screen currently displayed. This will contribute to their feeling of not being in control and increase their frustration. There are two frequently used ways to instruct the user to leave the display:

1. Put a prompt on the bottom of the display such as:

```
            Press RETURN to continue
                       or
            Press F2 for more help
```

2. Put a status message on the screen that indicates the action that will result from important keys such as:

```
    F1=Main Menu, F2=Previous Screen, F3=Next Screen
```

Be sure that the instructions you give are clear and specific. Don't say "Quit" when you mean "Return to Main Menu" or "Previous Screen."

When displays continue over multiple screens, the screen should indicate where the user is in the display.(6-6)

Many times the information being displayed such as a long list of items or a series of help screens cannot be shown on just one screen. This constraint is usually handled in two different ways:

1. The display is broken up into a number of screens that are each shown sequentially. Each screen is analogous to a page. When this approach is used, put a message such as "Screen 1 of 3" on each screen.

2. The user can scroll through the display rather than page through it. The scrolling is done in several ways, such as with arrow keys or with a mouse. If the display is a long one, there

should be some indication to users where they are in the display. Some computer systems have a "scroll bar" available. A scroll bar is an indicator, usually on the extreme left-or right-hand side of the display, that shows where the user is located in the data. For example, if the user is halfway through the data, the scroll bar is in the center of the screen. As the user moves closer to the end, the bar moves closer to the bottom of the screen. If your computer system allows you to display a scroll bar, use it in this way to show users where they are in a display. Be sure also to allow the user to leave the display at anytime. (See the previous guideline.)

Consider the skills of your users and the information they will manipulate when you display information in multiple windows.(6-7)

Windows are a relatively new and increasingly popular feature of software products. They provide users with the ability to display several "screens" of information at the same time. Users, however, must often pay a price for this capability: they must manipulate the window's placement and size.

Because windows are a recent phenomenon, there has not been much research on how to use them effectively. One recent study, however, does provide some insight into the complexity of the use of windowing systems (Bly and Rosenberg 1986). In this study, two types of window management systems, tiled windows and overlapping windows were compared. Tiled windows do not overlap. You can see all of the information in every window. The software, not the user, determines where to put tiled windows. Overlapping windows maximize the visibility of the information in the last, active window displayed by showing it in the foreground, overlapping the other windows. The user then has the ability to reposition and change the size of any window.

In this study, both new and experienced users of windows were asked to perform two types of tasks, one that required frequent manipulation of information between windows and one that did not. The results showed that experienced window users were faster at using overlapping windows for the task that required frequent window manipulations. New users, however, were faster at all tasks when they used tiled windows. When the new users had to use the overlapping windows, they spent much of their time manipulating the size and placement of the windows. Apparently, it takes a good deal of time to learn how to manipulate overlapping windows.

Surprisingly, nineteen out of the twenty-two subjects in this study preferred the overlapping windows, even when they performed faster with the tiled ones. Obviously, more research is needed to clarify the effectiveness of windows. But this study suggests that tiled windows may be more effective for applications that will be used by people who do not have experience manipulating windows. For a detailed discussion of tiled windows, see Cohen, Smith, and Iverson (1986).

DISPLAYING TEXT

The guidelines in this section are concerned with the effective display of text on the screen. They are primarily concerned with displays that contain running text, such as messages, help screens and tutorials.

Display text conventionally in mixed, upper and lower case and with appropriate punctuation. Put a blank line between each paragraph and double space text whenever you can.(6-8)

In my experience, the use of upper case text and the overuse of highlighting are the most frequent violations of the guidelines contained in this chapter. Apparently because they feel that it gives text greater emphasis, many programmers put everything in upper case, including menu options, titles, messages, and even help text. Yet, there is ample evidence that people read lower case text at a faster rate (Tinker 1963).

The research literature also shows that when people read, they do not look at the individual letters in a word but they see the whole word as a pattern. Have you ever been unsure of the spelling of a word and written it out so that you can "see" how it looks? If you have, you were relying on your ability to recognize the correct spelling through the pattern of the letters. Try doing it sometime by writing the word in upper case letters. You will find that the pattern is destroyed. The uniform size of the letters and the fact that none of them go below the line make upper case words relatively patternless.

Use upper case words only when you need to highlight them. Column and row headings can be displayed in upper case to separate them visually from the body of a table. (See Guideline 6-12.) Short titles can also be in upper case. Most all other text should be in lower case with initial capitals. Also you should display prose just as you would on paper, with proper punctuation within and at the end of sentences.

Because of the poor contrast on screens relative to paper documents, it will help users to read and to keep their place in text displays if you put a blank line between each paragraph of text. One of the important components of the skill of reading is keeping your place in the text. Writing short paragraphs and separating them visually helps readers, especially poor readers, to keep their place. In addition, research studies show that reading text on a video screen is ten percent faster when it is double-rather than single-spaced.

Left justify text but leave a ragged right margin.(6-9)

The widespread use of word processors now makes it possible to format text easily in a variety of ways. There is evidence from research studies, however, that indicates that the best way to format text is to simply left justify it. Do not justify the right margin. There are two reasons for this practice.

1. The text will end up with either uneven spacing between words (see Exhibit 6-2) and/or frequent hyphenation. If you have a long word at the end of a line of text and you are right justifying it, the word processor will usually put the word on the next line and add spaces between words on the previous line to make the spacing look even. This uneven spacing between words will slow down reading rates. In addition, when extra spaces are placed between the words of a paragraph, it can cause a "river" of white space that can distract the reader.

While there are no experiments that I am aware of that have compared the effect of justification on reading from a screen, there is ample evidence that right justification slows reading of text in paper

Exhibit 6-2   Effect of Right Justifying Text

```
This is an example of text that is not right
justified and, therefore, is easier to read because
the uneven right margin helps me to keep my place
in the text.


This is an example of text that is right justified
and, therefore, is harder to read because the even
right margin does not help me to keep my place in
the text.
```

form.   For example, Trollip and Sales (1986) found that right justification reduces reading rates by about ten percent, although it does not hamper comprehension of the meaning of the text. If you are interested in exploring this issue further, start with the excellent review by Mills and Weldon (1984).

2. Readers, especially poor ones, frequently "lose their place" in a paragraph of text. Right justification makes it harder for users to find it again.

Avoid hyphenation of words between lines.(6-10)

Hyphenated words are more difficult to read. They slow down reading rates, especially of poor readers. These words should be avoided. Hyphenating words between lines is a practice that most people tend to use only when they are typing with a conventional typewriter. I never hyphenate words when I am writing longhand, but when I type I frequently hear the bell go off when I have just started a long word. One of the great advantages of word processors is that I do not have to use the RETURN key at the end of a line so that I do not have to hyphenate at all.

If you use a word processor to create your text, you will not have to worry about hyphens unless you right justify your text. Some word processors will use hyphens in right justified text if you request it. Since I do not recommend right justifying text, you will not have any hyphenation problems if you follow this guideline and the previous one.

Use abbreviations and acronyms only when they are significantly shorter than the full text and when they will be understood by the user.(6-11)

Saving space by shortening the text is one of those trade-offs you often have to consider in implementing your design. The key to the guideline is its final phrase, "will be understood by the user." If some users will not understand the shortened form, then you should not shorten it. If you are certain that users will understand the shortened form, then it is permissible to use it, if you need the space. If you do not need the space, then only use the short form when it makes the   text flow more smoothly. For example, paragraphs are often more readable if you use the shortened form after the first instance of the long form rather than continually repeating the long form.

TABLES AND LISTS

Tables and lists provide an effective way to display data.   For example, if you are explaining a procedure to the user in three steps, indent the steps and number them.   This format will help the reader to locate and scan the steps, rather than trying to pick them out of a block of text.   The guidelines in this section describe a set of practices that will help you organize and format tables and lists. This organization will aid users in reading the displayed information and will assist them in finding the information they want. Table 6-1 shows a table of data on customer accounts. I will refer to this example throughout the discussion of the guidelines that follow.

Put a meaningful label, in upper case letters on the columns and, if appropriate, the rows of tables and lists. Continue the labels when a table or list extends over more than one screen.(6-12)

Notice that each of the columns in the example in Table 6-1 has a label.   These labels clearly describe the data displayed in each column.   In this example, the labels are highlighted by being displayed in capital letters and by being underlined. Several studies have shown that searching for individual words is faster when they are in upper case (Vartabedian 1971).

TABLE 6-1   EXAMPLE OF A DATA TABLE
Overdue Customer Accounts

NO.	CUSTOMER	ACCOUNT NUMBER	AMOUNT DUE	DATE DUE
1	Abbot, Mary	1750	550.00	11-07-84
2	Beaudet, Doug	1116	49.95	1-03-85
3	Carter, Owen	1254	62.49	12-24-84
4	Davis, Peter	917	350.00	12-24-84
5	Evans, Quincy	24	1550.50	10-12-84
6	Francis, Raymond	1815	163.35	12-30-84
7	Graham, Steven	1313	39.95	11-23-84
8	Hart, Tilly	1007	24.89	1-15-85
9	Iago, Ursula	556	0.99	1-02-85
10	Jones, Virginia	2116	890.79	12-30-84
11	Kelly, Walter	1654	69.99	12-01-84
12	Norris, Dana	1066	150.00	11-15-84

The labels are also separated from the body of the table by a blank line. If this table contained more items than are shown on this one screen, the labels would need to be present on all of the subsequent screens. This can be done in two ways:

1. If the data items are scrolled, the labels should be fixed on the screen and not be part of the scrolled area so that they remain in place as the body of the table changes.

2. If the additional items are paged on subsequent screens, the labels must be added to each of these screens.

Arrange the items in a table or list in some recognizable order to facilitate scanning.(6-13)

The alphabetical listing of customer names shown in Table 6-1 makes it easy for users to find information, if they know the customer's name. It obviously does not help if they know only the account number. That would require a different ordering. Every list of items should have some order that meets the user's needs.

Put items in a multiple column list in vertical columns which are read from left to right on the screen.(6-14)

When you have a long list of items to display, arrange the items so that users can read down the first column, then down the next column, etc. (See Exhibit 6-3.) Do not make the user read across the first row, then across the second row, etc. Vertical organization makes it faster to find an item (Parkinson and others 1985).

Left justify columns of alphabetic data; right justify columns of numeric data or align them by the decimal point or other delimiter.(6-15)

By properly aligning the columns of a table or list, you help the user to scan them quickly. The basic rules of alignment are

- Left justify alphabetic data
- Right justify integers
- Align fractional numbers or dollar values by their decimal points

• Align special fields such as dates or codes by their delimiters

The alignment of columns in Exhibit 6-2 illustrates these rules. The alphabetic listing of names is left-justified so that the first letters can be quickly scanned. The account numbers have been right-justified so that their relative sizes are quickly obvious. The dollar values in the AMOUNT DUE column are aligned by their decimal points, which makes it obvious which customers owe the most. Finally, the due dates have been aligned by the dashes between the month and day and between the day and year so that the column can be easily scanned.

Exhibit 6-3   List Organization

Organize lists vertically like this:

Adrian	Charles	Fatima
Agrippa	Glenda	Florence
Basil	Dana	Gordon
Beverly	Douglas	Hanna
Caine	Edith	Henry
Cary	Eliot	Hope

Rather than horizontally like this:

Adrian	Agrippa	Basil
Beverly	Caine	Cary
Charles	Glenda	Dana
Douglas	Edith	Eliot
Fatima	Florence	Gordon
Hanna	Henry	Hope

Try to find the name that is out of order in both lists.

Insert a blank line after about every fifth row in a long column.(6-16)

Reading long lists of items on a screen is similar to reading items on unlined paper. It becomes difficult to identify the row to which an item belongs. The problem is even worse on a video screen because of the relatively poor contrast the screen provides. Putting a blank line periodically in the table segments it visually into smaller blocks that make it easier to search for items and to identify the row in which they belong.

Put at least two spaces between the longest item in a column and the beginning of the next column.(6-17)

Because of the relatively poor contrast on video screens, it is important not to crowd information. Be sure that there is a clear visual separation between the columns of a table (See Parkinson and others 1985). Two spaces is about as close as two columns should get, three or four is better if you have the room.

Start with a "1" not a "0" when listed items are labeled by number.(6-18)

Only someone who is totally immersed in computer technology and who does not view software from the user's point of view would ever think of starting a list with a "0." Users expect lists displayed on the screen to start with a "1," just as lists in paper documents do.

Break up long strings of alphanumeric characters into smaller groups of three to four characters each.(6-19)

Occasionally, displayed lists contain items that are long strings of randomly appearing characters. Long telephone numbers or part numbers are examples. These strings should be broken up into smaller groups to facilitate readability. If there is a natural way to break up the strings, use it. For example:

6174115551   617-411-5551

When there are no natural breaks in the items, simply put a space between every three to four characters. For example:

87B7429G47   87B 7429 G47

HIGHLIGHTING

Highlighting refers to the practice of displaying information in special formats to emphasize its importance and to set aside special areas of the screen. Some of the common uses for highlighting are to indicate

- high priority messages or key words
- errors in data or entries

* warnings
* unusual data values such as those outside of recommended limits
* information that has changed or should be changed
* special areas of the screen

The following list shows most of the highlighting methods that are in common use:

* Blinking and audible tones
* Color differences
* Intensity differences
* Size differences
* Reverse video
* Boxing
* Font differences
* Underlining
* All capitals
* Position displacement

The meaning of these terms should be obvious, with the exception of "position displacement." This term refers to offsetting some items in a list by indentation to indicate that they are different from the other items. The guidelines that follow describe how to select an appropriate highlighting method and how to avoid the overuse of highlighting.

Use highlighting to emphasize important information only. Do not overuse it.(6-20)

The overuse of highlighting is one of the most common flaws in user interfaces. Some programmers seem to feel that it is necessary to emphasize everything on the screen that the user should read. There are three common ways in which highlighting is overused:

1. Using too much highlighting. Exhibit 6-4 is an example of a menu screen which contains too much highlighting. In this case, the designer has decided that the menu title, the menu options, and the prompt at the bottom must be emphasized on every menu screen. Showing this example on paper does not indicate how it looks on a screen. On the screen it has a" Christmas tree" effect on the viewer. You are not sure what to look at because so many things catch your eye. An ordinary menu does not need any highlighting with the possible exception of putting the title in capitals. Any screen, such as a menu, that appears repeatedly throughout an application does not need highlighting unless it contains an exception that the user should notice.

2. Using a more intense highlighting method than is needed. This abuse occurs when you use reverse video to highlight a label when displaying it in capitals would suffice or you blink an item when reverse video would do. (See the next guideline.)

3. Using highlighting to change the layout of the screen. As display technology becomes more advanced, this abuse is becoming more of a problem. Many designers feel that if color is available they should use it "to jazz" up the screen. I do not want to discourage you from designing a screen that is pleasant to look at and that focuses the user's eye on the critical information. But on a video screen, a little highlighting goes a long way, and it is very easy to use too much. Whenever you use any highlighting to make a screen look better, consider carefully each case to be sure that the highlighting has some purpose. Then verify its effectiveness in your usability tests.

Exhibit 6-4 Example of Overuse of Highlighting

                         Main Menu

        Options:
                  WP   Word Processing
                  EM   Electronic Mail
                  PH   Phone Directory

        Enter Option and Press RETURN:__

Use blinking and audible tones to highlight only critical information that requires an immediate response from the user. Turn them off as soon as the user has made that response.(6-21)

Blinking is, by far, the most intrusive form of highlighting. When not used appropriately, it is very annoying. It is so powerful that if it continues for any length of time, it forces people to look away from the screen. For software developed for an office environment, blinking should be used only in situations where the program will fail or stop and, as a consequence, data will be lost. In industrial or military applications, blinking may be used to tell operators that some critical event is taking place that requires their attention. When blinking is used, there should always be some means of turning off the blinking, preferably as soon as users make some response to indicate that they are taking appropriate action.

Make it clear what that action should be with a message. If you believe that the situation is so critical that you are going to make the information blink, then be sure to tell users how to resolve the situation.

Audible tones are frequently used to alert the user to the fact that an invalid key has been pressed or as an additional, redundant highlighting method when some critical message is being displayed. Tones can be effective if the user is likely to be looking at the keyboard or somewhere other than the screen. In my experience, tones are not as annoying to the user as they are to other people in the vicinity. I once had the opportunity to evaluate a program that sounded an audible tone every time the user was requested to make any input. I quickly learned to ignore the tones, but my colleagues in the office were not so fortunate. Use tones only when they are absolutely necessary and be sure to check their effectiveness during testing.

Select a highlighting method that is appropriate for the level of importance of the information being emphasized and for the layout of the screen on which it will be displayed.(6-22)

Each of the highlighting methods emphasizes information in a different way.   One of the important differences between the methods is the degree of emphasis that they give to the information being highlighted. The listing on page 99 shows the highlighting methods in what I believe is their approximate order of intrusiveness.   While you may quibble with the details of my ordering, there is no doubt that the methods near the top of the list will catch the attention of the user more quickly than those near the bottom. In fact, I see three levels of intrusiveness from most to least in this list:

- Level 1 consists of blinking and audible tones.
- Level 2 consists of color, intensity and size differences, reverse video, and possibly boxing.
- Level 3 consists of font differences, underlining, capitals, and position displacement.

Of course, the level of intrusiveness of a method is a function of how it is implemented on your equipment. Very small differences in size or intensity will not be very noticeable.   But, for most implementations, these three levels provide a good measure of the intrusiveness of a method.

I do not intend to tell you which highlighting method to use in every case. I can tell you, however, that the level of highlighting you will need is determined by at least two factors: (1) the importance of the information and (2) the layout of the screen on which the highlighting will appear.

1. Importance of the information. The previous guideline stresses the importance of reserving blinking and audible tones for critical information. Some examples of situations where you may consider blinking are (1) critical error and warning messages, (2) verification prompts that can lead to the destruction or alteration of data, and (3) important exceptions to normal practice. There are, however, very few cases where emphasis is needed which cannot be handled by a Level 2 highlighting method. The Level 3 methods are relatively weak visually. Consequently, they are best for displaying less critical items such as short titles, labels, headers, etc.

2. Screen layout. The degree of emphasis that a highlighting method gives to information is not absolute. It is influenced by the density of information on the screen and the highlighting that is already there. For example, displaying an error message in red is very intrusive if there are no other colors in the screen, but it may not be noticed on a screen filled with colors. You must see the highlighting on the screen on which it is to be used before you can be certain that it is appropriate for the importance of the information you wish to highlight.

When the user must read the information that is being highlighted, do not use a highlighting method which reduces the legibility of the information being emphasized.(6-23)

Several of the highlighting methods, such as blinking, reverse video, capitals, underlining, selected fonts, and certain colors, can actually reduce the legibility of the information being highlighted. (See the next guideline.) For example, a blinking message cannot be seen during the off part of the blinking cycle. If the message consists of a word or a short phrase, reading it may not be a problem. But a longer message may force the user to read it in pieces while the blinking cycle is on. One solution to this problem is to blink some other characters, such as asterisks, around or adjacent to the message. With the exception of blinking not all of the highlighting methods listed above will obscure a message in all cases. You will have to check each case to make sure that the information is clearly legible. If you have any doubt about its legibility, use another highlighting method.

Select colors from the center of the color spectrum. Select color combinations that complement each other.(6-24)

The effective use of color on video screens is an area of research that has not received the attention it deserves. I wish there were more guidance available on the use of color on video screens. The research literature, however, has very little to say on issues such as the "best" color in which to display information and the best mix of colors. In addition, human factors specialists have had only a few short years of experience using and evaluating color displays. Over the next few years, we will learn much more about the use of color.

Unfortunately, the psychology of color in not a simple area to understand or to research. The interrelationships among hue, brightness, intensity, contrast, and other variables are complex and are difficult for someone who is not a specialist in the area to understand. Furthermore, the appearance of colors can change from one manufacturer's display to another. If you are interested in learning more about how our visual system perceives color, start with the clear explanations provided by Murch 1984 and Taylor and Murch 1986.

It is very important that you do not overuse color in video screen displays. When you decide to add a color to the screen, you not only affect the perception of the information you are putting in color, but you may also be affecting the perception of other information on the screen. The human eye has to adjust itself constantly to focus on different colors. For example, when users move their eyes from a red object to a blue one, the muscles in the eye must adjust the lens to bring the blue object into focus. This process not only takes time but also can lead to eye fatigue if it occurs frequently.

The research literature, at the present time, seems to offer only a few rules that are of practical value:

Selecting colors

1. For a first choice, use a color from the middle of the color spectrum, such as yellow or green. Our visual system is most sensitive to these colors.

2. Don't use blue or magenta, a shade of pink, in displaying information that the user must read. Until recently the only

guideline that has repeatedly appeared in the literature has been to avoid the use of blue to display information. Because of the properties of the human eye, when all other factors are equal, blue characters appear dimmer than characters displayed in other colors. However, I have seen screens on which characters displayed in blue are just as legible as characters displayed in other colors. This may have been due to the mixture of some other color, such as green, with the blue. A recent study has also found magenta to be poor for displaying characters. In this study, characters displayed in magenta appeared washed out and adversely affected the subject's performance (Pace 1984). Therefore, if you display characters in blue or magenta, be very careful to check out their legibility. They may be fine, but there is growing evidence to indicate the characters may be difficult to read.

3. Use blue as a background color. The same factors that make blue a poor choice to display information that the user must read make it an excellent choice as a background color.

4. Avoid using red and green in the periphery of a display, particularly a large screen display. The sensors in the eye that detect red and green are concentrated in the center of the retina and are not present in its periphery.

Selecting color combinations

1. Use opponent colors, such as red and green or yellow and blue.

2. Avoid using color combinations from both ends of the color spectrum. Don't use red and blue or yellow and purple on the same screen. These combinations force the eye to adjust its focus as it moves from one to the other. The problem is worse when the colors are pure, that is, not mixed with other colors.

3. Avoid placing shades of blue beside each other. The eye has a difficult time detecting the edge of objects that differ only in the amount of blue.

Be consistent in the layout of displays and in the way that you highlight information.(6-25)

As with all the other components of the interface, consistency in the layout and highlighting of information is essential to making it easier to learn to use an application and to giving users the feeling that they know what to expect and are, therefore, in control.

Chapter 7

Entering Data

OVERVIEW

Effective data entry screens allow users to enter data quickly and efficiently. They help users to deal with one of the factors that makes communicating with computer software different from communicating with people, namely, the concern with the format, order, and exact spelling of information rather than its meaning. The guidelines are grouped into three broad categories: the layout of data entry screens, the design of data fields within screens, and the procedures to move within and between screens.

- Laying out the screen. The first three guidelines describe how to organize the entry screen. Data fields need to be grouped into logical categories or according to the structure of a paper form, when there is one.
- Structuring data fields. The next seven guidelines are concerned with the design of the data fields themselves. They describe how to format and word captions, indicate the size of fields, and provide context-sensitive help for data fields.
- Designing flexible procedures. The final six guidelines present techniques to allow users to be as free and flexible in entering data on a video screen as they would be in filling out a paper form. Users should be able to move freely through the fields on a screen and between screens, using a set of functions keys that execute one and only one function consistently.

Alfred Turing, the mathematician, designed a test which will allow us to tell when computers become as intelligent as people (Turing 1950). Imagine that you are in a room with a computer terminal. With this terminal you can ask questions of either a computer or a human being. Can you devise a question or questions that will allow you to distinguish between them by their answers? If not, the computer has passed Turing's test and is intelligent.

Of course, at the present time, telling the difference would be easy. One of the quickest ways to see the difference is to ask the computer and the person to ask you a question that you must answer correctly, such as "Ask me who the first president of the United States was." Assuming they can both ask you the question, there are literally hundreds of ways to answer it. The person should understand all of them. For example:

Washington
G. Washington
Geo. Washington

General Washington
General G. Washington
Washington, G.
Washington, Geo.
Washington, George
Washington, General
Washington, General G.
The man for whom the nation's capital is named

The computer software that is usually designed for data entry operations would have a hard time recognizing most of these responses as correct. It probably would have the least trouble with "Washington, George," which is not the form that people ordinarily use when talking with each other. The fact is that people who live in the same culture share a set of assumptions and rules that they depend on when they communicate. For example, no one would mistake "George" in this context for the last name of the president. Furthermore, as two people get to know each other, they use their shared experiences to facilitate their communication even further. For example, one person may say to another, without any apparent context, "I saw John today." The other person will know who John is and may also know why meeting him has special significance.

I have often taught classes of students who are new to computers. Sometime during the first class, a student sitting at a terminal or microcomputer will say, "This computer is dumb!". Invariably, the student's frustration is prompted by software that cannot recognize a response that a person easily could, such as typing "YIS" instead of "YES" or even "yes" instead of "YES." People are simply not used to worrying about the form of their communications. It is the meaning that usually counts, and other people understand this.

These examples illustrate the point that, given the present state-of-the-art in software technology, programs are not very sophisticated or flexible at understanding us, especially when we have data to communicate. Because the software cannot interpret our meaning, it forces us to be very exact in the order and form of our communications. Deviations, sometimes even slight ones, are often not recognized.

Perhaps someday, with advances in artificial intelligence, your software will be able to interpret some of the meaning of the information it processes. Until then you will have to help users do something that is very unnatural to them - to pay attention to the details of the data they enter, such as its order, format, and exact spelling. As we will see in this chapter, you can help users by laying out the screen so that it is clear which data should be entered. You accomplish this by designing data entry fields so that the order and form of data is obvious. In addition, you can provide the user with the flexibility to move easily within and between data entry fields and screens, and allow them to proceed at their own pace.

In this chapter, we will focus on the design of screens that are intended to allow the user to enter several data values. The entry of single values is covered in the next chapter, in the section on prompts. The guidelines that follow are grouped into three categories: the layout of data entry screens, the design of data entry fields, and the design of procedures by which users move both within and between data entry screens.

LAYING OUT THE SCREEN

The first three guidelines are concerned with the placement and arrangement of data entry fields on the screen.

When the user must transcribe data directly from a paper form to the screen, the layout of the screen should be similar to the layout of the paper form.(7-1)

Some data entry processes are simply transcriptions of data from a paper source document to the screen. In those cases, it is best to design the layout of the screen so that it is similar to the layout of the paper source document. For an excellent discussion of how to format such data entry screens, see Galitz (1981). If you design many data entry screens, I recommend purchasing Galitz's book.

Occasionally you will find that the paper document is so poorly designed that it makes it difficult to design an effective data entry screen. When this happens, there is usually no satisfying way to help the user. It would be nice to have the paper form redesigned, but this is rarely possible. The only advice that I can give you is to do the best you can to minimize the worst layout problems by following the other guidelines in this chapter.

Group data fields into logical categories on the screen; provide a header that describes the contents of each category.(7-2)

Exhibit 7-1 shows a poorly designed data entry screen. We will be examining the problems with this screen throughout the chapter.

Exhibit 7-1 An Example of a Poorly Designed Data Entry Screen

```
DATA FOR 016 FILE

NAME:
ACCT #:
ITEM NUM:
DESC:
AMOUNT:
PHONE:
ZIP:
STATE:
PAYMENT:
PURCHASE DATE:
TODAY'S DATE:
```

Two of its problems are violations of guidelines in Chapter 6. The first is that the title of the screen is informative only to the programmer. (See Guideline 6-1.) The title refers to the internal file name into which the data will be stored and thus is confusing to the user. Second, all the data entry fields are pushed over to the left-hand side of the screen. This practice is commonly done by some programmers for their own convenience, and since there is no symmetric balance to the display, it violates display Guideline 6-4.

There is no obvious order to the items in this display. While it is difficult to tell from the poor captions on this screen, there seem to be two categories of data: data that describes the customers and data that describes the purchase the customer made. Data from both these categories is randomly interspersed on this screen

Exhibit 7-2 shows an improved version of the screen displayed in Exhibit 7-1. Notice that it has a meaningful title and uses the whole screen to display the fields. In addition, the data fields have been grouped into two categories, customer description and purchase description, and each category has a header that describes it. This layout makes it clear to the user that there are two types of data and also makes it easier to scan the screen to find a particular field.

Make areas of the screen not needed for data entry or commands inaccessible to the user.(7-3)

You should control the cursor on a data entry screen so that it can move only within and between data entry fields and to the

Exhibit 7-2   An Improved Data Entry Screen

```
             Over the Counter Parts - 10/28/86

                    CUSTOMER DESCRIPTION


    NAME:_____        _____      __
               LAST                   FIRST            MI

    ACCOUNT NO:_____        PHONE:___-___-____

    STATE:__                     ZIP CODE:_____



                    PURCHASE DESCRIPTION


    ITEM NO:___-_____     DESCRIPTION:_____

         AMOUNT:$____.___     DATE(MM/DD/YY):__/__/__

         FORM OF PAYMENT(X):CASH_ CC_ CHECK_
```

command line, if there is one. For example, the user should not be able to move the cursor with the arrow keys and then change a caption or a screen title.

STRUCTURING THE DATA FIELDS

The next seven guidelines are concerned with the design of the fields into which the user enters data.

Never require the user to enter information which is already available to the software or can be computed by it.(7-4)

The user should not have to enter information that can be obtained from a system function or some other software component. The example of the poorly designed screen shown in Exhibit 7-1 asks the user to provide today's date. The improved example displays the date at the top of the screen. The data is provided by the software and displayed without having to ask the user for it. In many applications, users begin by accessing a data base and identifying the record on which they wish to work. This may be done by entering the number and title of the record. But, if the title can be supplied by the software based on the number alone, do not make the user enter both. Fill it in on the screen.

Do not require the user to enter dimensional units.(7-5)

If the user is entering dollar values, the "$", if used at all, should be placed automatically in the field by the software. The AMOUNT field in Exhibit 7-2 is an example. Most of the time, the dimensional symbols do not have to be used on data entry screens at all. They are usually needed only for report screens or printed reports. A word processor I frequently use allows me to print out copies of my work in single, double, or triple space. To select the spacing I want, however, I am forced to enter the letters "LI" for "lines" after I enter the number of lines I want it to space. I frequently forget to add the "LI" to the field and the software reminds me that my format is invalid by displaying a message. This unnecessary annoyance could have been avoided if the designer had eliminated the need to enter the letters in the first place.

Allow the user to enter data by character replacement.(7-6)

A complete data entry field consists of a caption and a block of space into which the user types the data. For example:

```
PROJECT NO.: _ _ _ _
```

In this case the user enters data by replacing the underscores with data values. The number of underscores should be equal to the exact number of characters to be entered, when you know what that number is, or to the maximum number of characters allowed in the block. For example, if the data to be entered is a name, you cannot predict how many letters will be entered, but you must indicate the maximum number allowed.

Underscores are not the only symbols that can be used as characters to be replaced. Sometimes there is a default value already in the field. The user can either replace the characters or tab over the field to accept the default.

Some programs that I have used put the data field in reverse video. There is a potential problem with this technique. If any of the user's equipment has a block cursor, the reverse video can cause the cursor to look as if it has disappeared. Basically this happens because the cursor is moved to the first character of the field. The cursor is already in reverse video. This reverses the reverse video of the first character of the field and makes it look like the cursor is not on the screen. For example, the data entry field shown above will look like this in reverse video:

PROJECT NO: ██████

The cursor is really there in the first position, but users can't see it. The first time this happened to me, I thought there was a bug in the program. I'm sure your users will be equally confused.

Put a caption describing the data to be entered adjacent to each data field; incorporate memory joggers into the caption.(7-7)

The caption is a word or phrase that describes the data to be entered. For example:

START DATE: _ _ _ _ _ _

Notice that the caption, START DATE, is in all capital letters for emphasis and is separated from the data field by a symbol, in this case ":". Whichever symbol you choose to separate the caption from the data field, use it consistently in all your fields. The above example requests that the user enter a date. How would you enter the date? Would you put the month first or the day? The user could put "9JAN84" in the field. A date is an example of a data field where users need an aid to remind them of the format of the date. Here's an improved caption:

START DATE (MM/DD/YY):_ _/_ _/_ _

Occasionally one caption can be used for a number of data fields, as indicated by the following example:

REPORT DATES   (MM/DD/YY)
          : __/__/__
          : __/__/__
          : __/__/__

Whenever a series of data entry fields is arranged in a column, you will have to decide whether to left justify or right justify the captions. Your objective should be to minimize errors by keeping the captions as close to the data field as possible. When the captions are of similar length, left justify them. For example:

```
Program Number  :   _ _ _ _ _ _
Project Number  :   _ _ _ _ _ _
Contract Number :   _ _ _ _ _ _
```

When the captions differ widely in length, right justify them. For example:

```
   Project Number :  _ _ _ _ _
University Number :  _ _ _ _ _
           Status :  _ _ _ _ _
```

Justify data entries automatically.(7-8)

Do not make the user enter leading or trailing zeros or blanks. For example, if the data field will accept numbers from 1 to 100, the user should be able to enter 5 instead of 005. Similarly, if dollar values are being entered, the user should not have to enter zeros for cents if there are none.

Display default values in data fields when appropriate.(7-9)

Occasionally, you will find a situation in which you expect the user to enter the same value most of the time. Unlike paper forms, data entry screens allow you to put in a default value that the user can accept by tabbing over the field. Use default values whenever you think they will be helpful. Make sure that the default value itself does not change when the user changes it. For example, if the default value is "yes" and the user types in "no," the next user should still see the original default "yes."

Provide context-sensitive help for data entry fields.(7-10)

I will be discussing help in Chapter 8. But it is worth mentioning here that data entry fields are one of the places where context-sensitive help is most effective. The term "context-sensitive" means that when the user requests help, the application software knows what information the user needs from the context of the request.   For example, the word processing software that I frequently use has a data entry screen that allows me to enter the values that I want to use to print out documents.   I can never remember the model number of the draft printer I normally use. The software, however, allows me to press an arrow key to get a list of the printers and then to tab over to the one I want. Without this feature I would have to write the model number on a piece of paper and tape it to my terminal. This is an example of context-sensitive help on a data entry field.

The help that you provide on a data entry field need not be this elaborate. It can be just a reminder of a format or of the meaning of the caption. See the discussion of the design of help in Chapter 8 for further information of the planning and design of help.

DESIGN FLEXIBLE PROCEDURES

The final set of guidelines in this chapter is concerned with the design of the procedures users must follow to move back and forth within a data entry screen and to move onto and off of that screen. It will help you to understand the importance of these procedures if you consider what it is like to fill out a paper form. When you apply for a loan or a new job, you are asked to fill out forms on which you provide a variety of information. When you fill out these forms, you usually can start wherever you wish, move freely from one field to another and from one page to another, and go back to any item that you filled out incorrectly to fix it.   You may even leave an item temporarily blank, such as your auto registration number, go out to your car to get it, and then come back to fill it in.

An important objective in designing effective data entry procedures is to allow users to be as free and flexible as they would be in filling out a well-designed paper form. In order to achieve this objective, you will have to design procedures that will help users to move freely between and within screens, and to edit and re-edit fields until they are satisfied with their entries. The guidelines that follow indicate the capabilities you should design into your procedures and provide some help in implementing them.

Allow the user to move freely through the fields in a data entry screen. (7-11)

Up until a few years ago, it was much more difficult to design flexible data entry screens because you could not allow the user to work with a whole screen of data at once. This was cumbersome for both the designer and the user. The designer had to treat each entry as if it were a separate screen, and the user had to wait for a response from the application program after each entry. In a multi-user environment, this process made response time slow.

With the advent of full-screen editors, these problems have evaporated. These editors allow users to enter a complete screen of data, edit it until they are satisfied, and then transmit it to the application program. These editors can even do some simple editing of data the user is putting on the screen without having to interact with the application program. This feature is such an advance over the older mode of line-by-line interaction that you should always use it if your computer system makes it available. If it does not, then try to come as close as you can to allowing the user the flexibility described in this and the following two guidelines.

The most important procedure to incorporate into the design of your data entry screens is the capability to move freely back and forth through the fields on a screen. If there are only a few fields, for example five or fewer, you can implement this guideline by simply allowing the user to move serially back and forth through the fields one at a time. If the screen, however, contains many fields, you will need to provide some additional capabilities, such as being able to move to the first data field at any time or to move to the top or bottom of a long list.

Allow the user to work on the whole data entry screen before transmitting the data to the application program. (7-12)

This is another feature of full-screen editing that frees users to work with the whole screen as a unit and to transmit it to the application software only when they are satisfied with it. This capability also frequently speeds up the data entry process because each data field does not have to be individually transmitted to the application software. Consequently, control is not constantly back and forth from the software to the user.

Allow the user to leave the data entry screen without filling in any data. (7-13)

This guideline is similar to Guideline 5-6 for menus and 6-5 for display screens. All three of these guidelines require that users be able to leave a screen at any time. It is extremely frustrating for users to be stuck on a data entry screen when they retrieved it by mistake and then be forced to enter some meaningless data before they can exit from the screen. Provide users with a means to leave the screen without needing to enter any data.

Each key used in a data entry screen should have one and only one function.(7-14)

This guideline leads into a discussion of functional capabilities that should be provided on a well-designed data entry screen and how to map the functions to keys. For this discussion, I am going to ignore the use of a mouse or a touch screen, since these devices are not very effective for data entry screens.

Table 7-1 shows a list of the capabilities that can be provided on a data entry screen. This list does not exhaust the possibilities, but, as you can see, there are many capabilities to consider. If you are going to provide the user with the flexibility that is required by the previous three guidelines, you may not always need all of them, but you will need many of them.

With the exception of the TAB key to move forward through the fields and the DELETE key to remove the character to the left of

TABLE 7-1 Data Entry Screen Functional Capabilities

Cursor Control Capabilities

- Move the cursor forward to the next data field
- Move the cursor backward to the previous data field
- Move the cursor to the first or some other designated data field
- Move the cursor forward one character in a field
- Move the cursor backward one character in a field

Editing Capabilities

- Delete the character to the left of the cursor
- Delete the character under the cursor
- Delete the whole field

Exit Capabilities

- Transmit the screen to the application program
- Move to another screen
- Confirm the saving of edits and go to another screen

Help Capabilities

- Get help on a data field
- Get help on a full screen

---

the cursor, I have not seen any consistency in the mapping of function keys to functions. Each design team seems to create their own. You can avoid inconsistency in your procedures by writing them down in the user-interface handbook I discussed on Chapter 3. You and your colleagues need to agree on a set of conventions for data entry procedures and put them into the handbook so that everyone can follow them.

Provide users with either a status message on the data entry screen or a help message that shows the mapping of keys to functions. (7-15)

Users need to know which keys have been assigned to the functions discussed in the previous guideline. This is especially important for new users and for users who do not frequently do data entry. If there are many function keys that an application uses in addition to the data entry procedures, a printed Quick Reference Guide is often used to supplement online information. However, users frequently need some online information about the use of special keys. There are two types of messages that can be used to convey this information. First, a status message can be displayed, usually at the bottom of the screen, listing the functions of the keys. For example:

```
F2=Help   F3=Main Menu TAB, BACKTAB
```

Second, a help message can be provided that describes the functions of the keys and also shows their location.

Be consistent in the design of data entry screens, fields, and procedures. (7-16)

As is the case with all the design features described in this book, consistency in the design of data entry screens and procedures is essential. Use the same words to describe the fields and functions; use the same format for your screens; assign each special key to one and only one function; and use the same procedures to move within and between screens.

Chapter 8

Smoothing Communication With Online Documentation

OVERVIEW

Online documentation consists of a set of techniques to smooth the communication between a software application and its users. These smoothing techniques allow users to carry on an effective dialogue with the application. General guidelines, which apply to all types of online documentation, are presented. They suggest that you use plain English in messages and avoid attempts at humor in messages. The twenty-four specific guidelines cover four types of messages: status messages, prompts, error messages, and help messages.

- Status messages are important for giving users the feeling they are in control of the software. They tell users what the software is doing, where they are in the sequence on screens, what options they have selected, and what options are available.

- Prompts ask the user to type data or commands or to make a simple choice. Memory aids used in a prompt help users to type their response in the proper format and order.

- Error messages should allow users to recover from mistakes by making it clear what the mistake was and how to correct it. Error messages need to be specific about why a mistake was made without blaming users for the problem.

- Help messages are typically requested by users when they want to perform a new, complex, or infrequently used procedure, or when they do not know what else to do. The text of help messages needs to be planned, drafted, and evaluated as carefully as print documentation. In addition, the layout and format of help must be designed to deal with the special constraints imposed by the video screen.

In the 1960s, when I was first learning to use a computer, I punched commands onto cards and batched them together with a set of job control cards to tell the computer who I was and what I wanted to do. In return, I received a printout that contained some status information and the results of my run. In those days, much of the difficulty in learning how to get the computer to help me came from this indirect form of communication. When something went wrong it was difficult to find out what caused the problem. Often human intervention was the only way to solve it. This usually meant requesting a "core dump" and then bringing it to an expert who could interpret the octal numbers and tell me what the problem was.

With the 1970s and the introduction of time-sharing computers, communication with an application became more direct. I could then sit at a teletype machine loaded with heavy yellow paper and type my commands one at a time. The results of the run would be typed line by line on the paper. While I was told this was a great advance over the batch card mode of communication, I was, at first, more comfortable with my cards than with the teletype. I now know that my uneasiness with time-sharing was caused by the lack of status messages, prompts, effective error messages, and online help. I can still remember sitting at the teletype and not having a clue about what I should do next. I didn't know if the computer was down or why I kept getting the same incomprehensible error message when I was "obviously" doing everything correctly.

The days of the teletype are gone, but the problems of communicating with software remain. The applications I now use are much more powerful than ever before. They are faster and more efficient, and they provide more functionality; but I still often have trouble using them. Why? I believe the problem stems from a fundamental lack of understanding about the nature of computer software. There are two tasks that you, the designer, must do to create an effective application. First, you must construct software that contains a basic functionality that allows people to get some job done. Second, you must also surround this functionality with a set of procedures and messages that allow the user to carry on an effective dialogue with the application. A major component of designing from the user's point of view is designing this dialogue process so that it runs smoothly and efficiently.

As you will see later in this chapter, when two people are working together to get some task done, their conversation is filled with instructions which relate to the details of the task at hand. These instructions are surrounded by words, messages, gestures, and other nonverbal cues that serve the purpose of smoothing the communication process. These smoothing mechanisms do such things as indicate who is in control of the conversation, when control is passed from one person to the other, when it is appropriate to interrupt, when to be cautious, and when mistakes have been made. These mechanisms are not part of the task to be performed but rather are used to smooth the communication process. Without them it would be difficult, if not impossible, to get the task done.

Online documentation is nothing more than a set of techniques to smooth the communication between an application program and the user. Titles, headers, status messages, prompts, error messages, and help text serve the purpose of aiding users to communicate and work with the functionality an application contains. They make the critical difference between an application that is easy to learn and use and one that is frustrating and prone to error.

Unfortunately, most design engineers have had a minimum of training in communication techniques. They understand the technical challenge in designing an application as one of structuring a database or a set of modules to provide the user with a set of functions, but not in the communication techniques that surround these components and make them easy to use. For this reason, this chapter is the longest in the book and contains guidelines that deal with the fundamentals of both planning and creating online documentation. Much of the information in this chapter is likely to be new to you because it is an aspect of interface design that is the farthest from most software designer's training. I believe, however, it is the missing factor that, when combined with an effective application, makes the difference between an enjoyable and productive experience and a frustrating and wasteful one.

THE SCOPE OF ONLINE DOCUMENTATION

The term "online documentation" is a relatively new one in the user-interface literature. It was not used with any frequency until the 1980s and there is no standard definition for it. On the surface, the term appears to refer to documentation that is presented on a video screen. To put it another way, "online" refers to the medium on which the documentation is presented. Therefore, "online documentation" can refer to the literal translation of paper documentation onto a computer screen. In some cases this has been done. We know, however, that when printed documentation is taken literally from paper to screen, it loses its effectiveness. Reading text on a video screen is different from reading it on paper. We will explore this difference throughout this chapter.

Rather than trying to define online documentation, let's look at examples of it:

Screen Titles
Captions
Headers
Messages
    Status Messages
    Prompts
    Error and Warning Messages
Help
Tutorials

This is a list of the full range of online documentation. Some organizations include all of these in their definition because they believe the term refers to all of the words a programmer or writer creates to display on the screen. Other organizations restrict the term to help and tutorials because these components are the closest to their view of the essence of paper documentation, namely descriptive prose.

We have already discussed screen titles, captions, and headers at length in Chapter 6. In this chapter, we will concentrate on messages and help. Tutorials are beyond the scope of this book. Most of the guidelines in this chapter do apply to tutorials, but you will need more guidelines than I will describe here to be able to create an effective tutorial.

I believe that writers should be creating all online documentation. A programmer can create the first draft of messages and menus and review them for accuracy, but the writer should then take over and also create all of the online help and tutorials. It has been proven that software specialists have difficulty creating effective online documentation. Later in this chapter we will see examples that demonstrate this point. Furthermore, as much as I hate to admit it, human factors specialists are not always good writers either. Writers are simply better at this job than other professionals. They have training and experience that the rest of us do not have. In Section I, we saw how important it is to have a writer on your software development team and how that writer needs to work together with you to view the software from the user's perspective. You will see in this chapter what a critical role the writer plays in the interface development process.

A SCREEN IS NOT A PIECE OF PAPER

Throughout this book, we have seen the similarities and differences between video screens and paper. In this section we will look at this comparison in more detail.

Even though you have read many books, you may never have considered the characteristics of a book that make it easy to find the information you want. Perhaps the biggest advantage a book has is that you can pick it up and manipulate it. You can easily skim through the pages. You can go to the front to look at the table of contents or to the back at the index. These features make it especially easy to look quickly to see if the book contains the categories of information you need. Each page in a book also contains a large amount of information. It is not unusual for an average sized book to have 45-60 lines of text on each page and 70-85 characters per line. Furthermore, most textbooks have black print on white pages, which provides the high contrast that makes reading easy and fast.

There are, however, some disadvantages to book format. The book is not always available when you need it, and a specific piece of information in the book is often difficult to find. For example, I was recently looking in my word processing manual to learn how to double-space a document. There was no entry in either the table of contents or the index under "double space." After some extensive searching, I found that the information about double-spacing a document is hidden in the section on formatting paragraphs.

Online documentation, if done well, can overcome the disadvantages of paper documentation. It is always available and you can ask for only what you need. In addition, it can also be displayed on the screen with the work you are doing. Online documentation, however, does have its limitations. You cannot skim through a series of screens as quickly as you can the pages in a book. In addition, you cannot display very much information on a screen because

1. A screen is smaller than a page. Most screens limit you to about 20 lines.

2. A screen has relatively poor contrast. Consequently, reading rates for text are slower on a screen than on paper. A text paragraph that looks easy to read in a book will look longer and more crowded on a screen. Several recent studies have shown that reading continuous text on a video screen is about 25 percent slower than reading the same information from a book (Kruk and Muter 1984; Muter and others 1982). It now appears that this phenomenon is due to the poor legibility of the characters themselves (Gould and others 1986).

3. People are often put off by a packed screen of information. In my experience many managers will not even begin to read a help screen that is filled with text.

These constraints make it important that you plan your online documentation carefully. You will have to be much more clever in organizing, formatting, and choosing your words to create effective online documentation than you would in conveying the same information on paper. Later in this chapter, we will be discussing the steps you will need to follow to plan, create and edit online documentation. The guidelines and examples in this chapter should help you to follow these steps and to create better online documentation.

GENERAL GUIDELINES

In this section, we will discuss some guidelines that apply to all types of online documentation. Rather than repeating them several times throughout the chapter, they will be presented here once, and I will then refer back to them when necessary.

Write online documentation in plain English.(8-1)

This and the following three guidelines are concerned with the language you use in designing the interface. (See Dumas and Redish 1986.)

Plain English is writing that is

- straightforward and reads as if it were spoken
- clear, direct, and simple
- effectively organized with a concern for what users need to know

Plain English does not

- limit you to one-or two-syllable words or short phrases and sentences
- write down to users or treat them in a condescending manner

While essayists and writing specialists have been urging us to use plain English for more than thirty years (Chase 1953), the plain English movement gained its momentum during the 1970s through a federal commission, presidential executive orders, and new laws and regulations on the federal and state level. These actions were the result of consumer activism and the growth in the amount of paperwork that new government programs were generating (Redish 1985).

A poor user interface exhibits many of the features of the poorly designed and written government and legal documents that led to the plain English movement. I have discussed many of these poor practices in Chapter 6, especially the use of uninformative titles and the inconsistent use of terms. The next three guidelines will focus on three other deficiencies: (1) not speaking directly to the user, (2) overusing nouns, and (3) using jargon.

Address the user directly as "you"; use the active voice.(8-2)

The way you address the user in your messages and help text is important in establishing the tone of the interaction between the user and the software. If you write online documentation in the third person, your software will appear to be as impersonal as a form letter. Consider the following two sentences:

- Three reports can be printed by the users of this program.
- You can print three reports with this program.

Readers of the first sentence get the impression that, as users, they are members of some abstract group that is being addressed. The second sentence addresses them directly. The first sentence is also more awkward because it is written in the passive voice. Often the use of the third person to address the user and the use of the passive voice occur together in online documentation. It is part of the style of many programmers. To avoid this style, address the user directly as "you" and minimize the use of the passive voice. But be careful about using "you" in error messages. (See Guideline 8-13.)

There is a good deal of controversy in the user interface literature about whether a program should ever use the first person, such as "I am working... ." Some experts believe that this practice should be forbidden. Their argument is that using "I" creates a distorted impression that the software is somehow human-like or at least alive. These writers believe this adds to many people's fear that somehow computers are mysterious machines with have magical powers. *2001: A Space Odyssey* dramatized this concept. While I sympathize with these writers, I am not yet ready to forbid the practice. I do not recommend the frequent use of the first person, but I do believe that whether we like it or not, every large software system has a persona that it conveys to the user. If you use the third person in your online documentation, users are likely to view your interface as impersonal. The judicious use of "I," along with the other practices described in this chapter can give your software a more personal feel. Don't overdo it, however, and see Guideline 8-6 on the use of humor.

Addressing the user directly in the second person is not the same as putting the user's name in messages. Some systems put the user's name on the initial screen after the user logs in. This is acceptable. The problem comes when you put names in interactive messages. I find this practice offensive. In a survey of professionals who use computers, they were asked whether they would "like a computer to generate sociable chit-chat" (Zoltan 1982). This question evoked the strongest negative response of any of the questions asked. Social chit-chat is one of the features that often occur in educational software. I get angry when I am using a program that starts with "Hi Joe! How are you today?" Avoid using the user's name in interactive messages.

Use simple action verbs to describe procedures. Don't use nouns to replace pronouns, verbs, and adjectives.(8-3)

One of the characteristics of interfaces that do not use plain English is that they use nouns to replace pronouns, verbs, and adjectives. The resulting communication is formal, impersonal, abstract, and difficult to understand. In the previous guideline we saw examples of using nouns to replace the pronoun "you." In addition, nouns are frequently used as adjectives to modify nouns, because noun strings often take up less space than the phrases that explain how the nouns fit together. Designers frequently write phrases such as "Production Database Maintenance," which obscure the action the user is to take. Beginning the phrase with a verb, such as "Maintaining the Production Database," would be clearer.

Finally, don't make nouns act as verbs.

Instead of:	Try these:
Modification	Modify or Change
Maintenance	Maintain or Keep
Selection	Select or Choose
A Pick	Pick or Choose

Describe procedures in logical order.(8-4)

Whenever you describe a procedure or a series of steps, put them in the order in which the user will execute them. For example, instead of

```
"Press the Enter key, but before you do, be sure that you
have saved your file or you may lose it,"
```

say

```
"Be sure to save your file before you press the Enter key."
```

Use simple English words, not computer or other jargon.(8-5)

This is one of the easiest guidelines to understand but one of the most difficult to implement, especially if you do not have writers creating your online documentation. We all live in a professional environment in which we spend most of our time interacting with people who have the same educational background and read the same books and journals. When we communicate, we use words and phrases that these people understand but that those outside of this community do not. Most of us have difficulty when we have to explain these words and concepts to others. At least three different types of jargon commonly occur in software interfaces:

- terms that are unique to the computer profession or to a particular company, such as "FILESPEC" or "ABEND"
- terms that have a common meaning outside of the data processing environment, but a special meaning within it, such as "BOOT," "ABORT," "DEFAULT," and "UTILITY"
- terms that are made up to describe some special function, such as "UNGROUP" and "DEARCHIVE"

Whenever you must use a term that is peculiar to your product or familiar only to software professionals, define it for the user in a short phrase or with help text.

Consider the two help screens shown in Exhibits 8-1 and 8-2. These screens are part of the help system of a large minicomputer in

Exhibit 8-1 Example Help Screen on Help

```
The HELP command invokes the HELP Utility to display information
about a particular topic.

The help utility retrieves help available in the system help files
or in any help library that you specify.  You can also specify a
set of default help libraries for HELP to search in addition to
these libraries.

Format:
                HELP [keyword [...]]

New users can display a tutorial explanation of HELP by typing TU-
TORIAL in response to the "HELP Subtopic?" prompt and pressing the
RETURN key.

For a more detailed description of HELP, type COMMANDS and press
the RETURN key.

Additional information available:

Tutorial  Commands  Parameters  Qualifiers
```

Exhibit 8-2   Example of More Help on Help

Commands

There are four different types of prompts in an interactive session, each representing a different level in the hierarchy of help available. The four prompt levels are:

1. If the root library is the main library and you are not currently examining help for a particular topic, then a prompt of the form "Topic?" is displayed.
2. If the root library is a library other than the main library and you are not currently examining help for a particular topic, then a prompt of the form "<library-name> Topic?" is output.
3. If you are currently examining help for a particular topic (and subtopics) then a prompt of the form "<keyword...> subtopic?" is output.
4. A combination of 2 and 3.

You can enter any one of several responses to these prompts. Each type of response, and its effect on HELP in each prompting environment, are documented in the table below.

RESPONSE		ACTION IN CURRENT PROMPT ENVIRONMENT
keyword [...]	(1,2)	Search all enabled libraries for the keys.
	(3,4)	Search additional help for current topic (and subtopic) for these keys.
@filespec [keyword [...]]	(1,2)	Same as above, except the root library is the library specified by filespec. If the specified library does not exist, then treat @filespec as a normal key.
	(3,4)	Treat @filespec as a normal key.
?	(1,2)	Display the topics available in the root library.
	(3,4)	Display list of subtopics of current topic (and subtopics) for which help exists.
CARRIAGE RETURN	(1)	Exit from HELP
	(2)	Change root library to main library.
	(3,4)	Strip the last keyword from list of keys defining current (sub)topic environment.
CTRL/Z	(1,2,3,4)	Exit from HELP.

an organization with which I recently worked. Typing HELP on that computer displays a list of commands on which help is available. One of the commands is HELP. When you type HELP HELP to get help on "HELP," the screen shown on Exhibit 8-1 is displayed. If you then follow the instructions on that screen and type COMMANDS and press RETURN, the screen shown in Exhibit 8-2 is displayed. I find it difficult if not impossible to make sense of these two help screens. We will talk more about help screens below, but the point here is to look for the words and phrases a naive user would have a problem understanding. The following is a partial list:

- HELP Utility
- System help file
- Help library
- Default help library
- Keyword
- Interactive session
- Prompt levels
- Subtopic
- Output
- Root library
- Main library
- Prompting environment
- Enabled
- Filespec
- Normal key
- Strip
- Topic environment

In addition to the examples of computer jargon that these two help screens illustrate, you will often find idiosyncratic words in online documentation, such as "ungroup" or "depaint."

Avoid humor in online documentation.(8-6)

While it is important to create a warm, positive tone with your online documentation, do not try to do it with humor. Humor is extremely difficult to create effectively. What is funny to one person is often insulting to another. There are some examples of humor that are effective, but most of the time it is forced and annoying. When I was a graduate student, I wrote a program which was widely used in my department. One of the error messages in the program began with the words "You idiot, you made a stupid mistake on card number... ." At the time I thought this message was funny. A few of the students who knew me personally did also, but most people were insulted and angered by the message. Fifteen years later I was introduced to a professional colleague who had attended the same school after I had left. When I was introduced, he reacted immediately to my name by saying "You are the one who wrote that program with the 'you idiot' message in it." He remembered little else about the program.

It is unlikely you would ever tolerate having such a blatantly insulting message in your software. Even milder attempts at humor can backfire. Avoid the possibility of this happening by not attempting humor. If you are really convinced you have created clever and effective humor, use it only after you have tested it thoroughly with potential users.

There are four additional general guidelines that also apply to online documentation which I discussed in Chapter 6 on text displays. These guidelines (6-8 to 6-11) stress the importance of displaying text in conventional upper and lower case, using a ragged right margin, avoiding hyphenation and using abbreviations sparingly.

DESIGNING MESSAGES THAT INFORM

In the chapter on general principles (Chapter 4), I discussed the importance of making users feel they are in control. The feedback a program provides is one of the important factors in conveying this feeling. The messages a program displays are responsible, to a large extent, for smoothing the communication between the user and the application. These messages ensure that control is passed freely back and forth from users to the software and keep users informed about processing status and their location in an application. Messages are usually short, from a few words to a few lines, and they are always initiated by the software. There are three types of messages I will discuss:

- Status messages
- Prompts
- Error or warning messages

To illustrate how these messages work in human conversation, consider the following sample dialogue between two people, Don and

Anna, using the telephone to pass information about a name and an address:

```
Don:    "Wait, I will get my pencil."(status)
Anna:   "OK."(status)
Anna:   "I'll wait."(status)
Don:    "OK."(status)
Don:    "Go ahead."(prompt)
Anna:   "OK."(status)
Anna:   "The name is J-A-N-E-D-O-E."
Don:    "J-A-N-E-D-O-E."(status)
Don:    "OK."(status and implied prompt)
Anna:   "OK."(status)
Anna:   "17 A-B-B-E-Y."
Don:    "Hold it!"(warning)
Don:    "E-Y"(status)
Don:    "Go ahead."(prompt)
Anna:   "OK."(status)
Anna:   "In Watertown. Did you get that?"(prompt)
Don:    "Yes.  Give me the zip on that."(prompt)
Anna:   "OK."(status)
Anna:   "I am looking it up."(status)
Don:    "OK."(status)
Anna:   "I have it."(status)
Anna:   "It's 09837."
Don:    "OK." (status)
Don:    "That's 09387."(status)
Anna:   "No!  It's 8,3 not 3,8."(error)
Don:    "OK."(status)
```

Notice how important the status messages are to the flow of this conversation. They let both participants know that information has been received and they also indicate that each person understands who is in control of the conversation and who should speak next. There is a lot more happening even in this simple conversation than is at first apparent. For example, notice that Anna did not have to indicate that Jane was the first name and Doe was the second because it was assumed the other person shared a common knowledge about names. Also, the end of the conversation that relates to the error about the zip code is quite cryptic, yet easily understood. Interchanges between computers and people are not usually so cryptic, and the format of data that is transmitted must be clearly specified. In the next three sections I will discuss further the similarities and differences between human-human and human-computer conversation. For a more detailed analysis on this issue see Nickerson (1981).

Describing What's Happening with Status Messages

As I stressed at the beginning of this chapter, online documentation is a set of procedures and messages that are added into and around the basic applications software to smooth the communication between the user and the application. As you will see, status messages are never required to run an application. They could all be eliminated and the application could still be operated. You could take all of the status messages out of the sample conversation on the previous page and the essential information about the name and address would still be there. In fact, the dialogue in novels is usually presented without such status messages. However, if you listen

Figure 8-1 Status messages give the user a feeling of control

to people talking, especially over the telephone, you will hear the types of status messages that are in the sample. They are critical to smooth communication. For this reason, an interface without status messages is difficult to use because it ignores the communication component of the dialogue with the user. As the designer of software, you must add these messages to your application to make it communicate with the user.

Use status messages to tell the user what the software is doing, where the user is in a sequence, and what options the user has selected or that are available.(8-7)

In general, status messages can be grouped into three categories, based on the type of status they convey:

Processing status
Option status
User location status

1. <u>Processing Status</u>. The following four examples tell the user about the status of processing:

```
Please Wait
I am storing the file
Filename: REPORT.DOC
Ready
```

The first two are common examples of messages that provide feedback that keeps the user informed about what actions the software is carrying out. The third example is an alternative form of a processing message. It echoes users' input and also tells them that their entry is being processed. It is displayed when the accuracy of data the user has entered is critical. This type of message is often combined with a prompt which requests the user to confirm the correctness of the entry. The fourth message is a relatively uninformative message. Unless it occasionally blinks, the user will not be sure processing is continuing.

There is another form of processing status message which is being used more frequently. It is the use of an icon to show processing status. Sometimes a clock which has hands that do not move is used. I have also seen a bee which buzzes around the screen at random used for this purpose. These icons convey the same information as a word message.

Processing status messages are often used to fill in the silent periods in a human-computer interaction. When two people talk over the phone, long silent periods are usually uncomfortable. These periods are often broken up by such phrases as "I'm still here." Computer users are also made uncomfortable by silent periods. When there are long periods between responses from the software, users begin to wonder whether the software is still in control and working or whether the conversation has been somehow broken off. In such situations the user usually presses the RETURN key, which is analogous to saying "Are you still there?" These uncomfortable periods can be avoided by the use of status messages.

Caution. Do not fill empty time with messages that describe the internal activities of the software in computer jargon such as

```
FORTRAN END
15 RECORDS PROCESSED*** 0ERRORS
LINK MAIN
```

Messages of this type give users the impression they are dealing directly with the internal workings of the computer instead of being shielded from them by the interface.

There is another technique for keeping users informed about the progress of processing. It is called a "percent-done indicator." It can take any one of several forms, such as a thermometer with percents on it, an hourglass, or a clock with a hand that points at percents instead of hours. The indicator shows the users not only that the software is working, but also, with a relatively continuous motion, what percent of the processing is done. As the processing continues, the indicator moves toward 100 percent. Myers (1985) has shown users prefer this type of indicator over having no other indication of processing status. Percent-done indicators seem to be especially useful for new computer users who frequently assume computers do everything quickly. Of course, you can only use these indicators when you know how long a process will take. This is sometimes possible in programs that query data bases.

Unfortunately, it may not always be clear to you during software development when processing status messages are needed. It is usually very late in the software development cycle when the need arises. Frequently, the development team proceeds under the assumption that the final product will run much faster than the development versions. These optimistic predictions sometimes are not realized until it is so late in the development process that it is difficult to put appropriate messages in the first release. In addition, many applications begin by having the user select an item to examine or update from a data base. There is often no way to know if it will take ten or twenty seconds to retrieve an item until the data base is fully loaded. This problem may not show up until usability testing or after. If testing of the interface is included early in the testing process, however, as was recommended in Section I, it should be possible to add these important status messages to the software.

2. Option Status. The following are examples of messages that inform the user of the options which have been selected or which are in effect:

```
CAPS is on
INSert on
Menu mode
```

This type of message is usually displayed in a consistent location on the periphery of the screen, such as the bottom or the upper right-hand side.

3. User Location Status. The following are examples of messages that tell users where they are in a process or in the structure of the application:

```
L15,C70
Screen 1 of 3
Menu 1.7
```

They express the user's location on a screen, in a linear sequence of screens, or in a hierarchy of screens. Because the user cannot skim through a software system as if it were a paper document, these messages are critical to giving users the feeling of being in control by knowing where they are at all times. For example, as we discussed in the section on menus, a message such as "Menu 1.7" is important when the menu structure is complex. As we will see in the discussion on help, messages such as "Screen 1 of 3" tell users how many help screens there are and which screen is being displayed. The format of these messages is telegraphic.

Prompting the User for Information

Prompts are short messages that ask the user to make a simple choice or to enter data or a command. In the early days of interactive software, there were many programs which were hastily converted from a batch environment, where there was no direct interaction with the user, to an interactive environment. Unfortunately, there were very few prompts added to these programs, probably because the programmers doing the conversion were not aware of the importance of the communications component of interactive processing. Consequently, users were forced to memorize the sequence and format of a series of inputs. Because people are poor at recalling details, errors were frequent and annoying. To cut down on the frequency of errors, it was a common practice to keep lists of commands on pieces of paper. Of course, I could never remember where the list was when I needed it. A few well-designed prompts would have saved me a lot of wasted effort.

Figure 8-2 Effective prompts help users to remember how to execute procedures

Use prompts to ask the user to make a simple choice or to enter data or commands. Be as specific as possible.(8-8)

Well-designed prompts are important because they are memory aids that reduce errors. Display a prompt when the user has to enter data or a command, or has to make a simple choice, such as between "Yes" or "No." Table 8-1 contains a list of typical prompt messages. Prompt messages are actually a form of online help. Rather than just displaying an uninformative symbol, such as "A>" and forcing users to ask for help when they are not sure what to do, a prompt indicates to users specifically what they should do next. Vague wording negates the effectiveness of a prompt. If you find yourself using words such as "data" or "information" in your prompt, you are probably not being specific enough to help the user. As with other forms of online documentation, address the user directly as "you," use either imperative or interrogative sentences, use "type" or "press" rather than "enter" or "hit," and use mixed, upper and lower case text.

TABLE 8-1   Examples of Prompt Messages

---

1. Type your password:_____
2. Type initiation date(MM/DD/YY):__/__/__
3. Do you want to save this file? Press Y or N._
4. Do you want to save this file?<Y>:_
5. Type menu option:__
6. Press RETURN to leave Help:_

Include memory aids in the prompt to make formats, infrequently used processes, or exceptions to normal practice clear.(8-9)

Since prompts are a form of online help, they should make it clear what form the user's response should take. As with all data entry screens, the format of items such as dates, codes, and filenames are particularly prone to error. Make it clear in the prompt what the user should do by including a memory aid in the prompt such as Example 2 in Table 8-1.

When defaults are allowed with prompts, indicate clearly which default value will be initiated.(8-10)

Example 4 in Table 8-1 shows a prompt with a default value. The user has three possible responses to this prompt:

1. Type "Y" to save the file.
2. Type "N" to not save the file.
3. Press RETURN to accept the default and save the file.

This format is often used in prompts that confirm some action, especially when one of the values is expected to be entered most of the time. The default makes it easier for the user by allowing the use of a more frequently used key, the RETURN key. However, the time that is saved is minimal.

Caution.   A default value should never destroy data or take any other action which cannot be reversed. If users walk away from the terminal and forget where they are or if response time is slow and the users are not sure whether they are connected, they will likely press the RETURN key. For this reason, the default should never allow the user to destroy data. For instance, Example 4 in Table 8-2 should never allow "NO" to be the default value.

Recovering from Errors

Error messages are almost always a surprise to me. They occur when I don't expect them and they tell me I did something wrong. They can also be an indication that I do not understand how to interact with the program and, therefore, am not in control. When the message is a poor one, that is, one that does not tell me what I did wrong and what to do about it, my reaction is one of anger at the software designer. I frequently condemn the whole program as a result.

Effective error messages allow users to recover smoothly from mistakes and make it clear why errors were made so that they are less likely to recur. Error messages, along with a help system, provide users with a safety net to catch them when they fall and put them back on the track to being productive. Table 8-2 shows some examples of poor error messages and also lists their characteristics. In this section I will refer to these examples and characteristics and discuss the guidelines that will help you to create more effective error messages.

Design your software to check for obvious errors.(8-11)

TABLE 8-2   Examples and Characteristics of Poor Error Messages

EXAMPLES

1. ERROR OPENING FILE
2. PROTECTION VIOLATION #367
3. MISCELLANEOUS PERMANENT ERROR
4. FATAL I/O ERROR
5. PROGRAM ABEND
6. EOF FOUND AFTER RECORD 139
7. SUMCHECK
8. WRONG CODE, TRY AGAIN
9. YOU ENTERED AN INVALID MONTH

CHARACTERISTICS

- Vague, contain meaningless codes.
- Blame the user.
- Have a negative tone.
- Attempt humor, but are insulting.
- Don't help solve the problem.
- All upper case reducing readability.

One of the beneficial effects you will achieve by designing a more effective interface is that users will make fewer errors. There are some types of errors, however, that can't be completely eliminated. People will misspell words, make typos, and transpose numbers. Making these kinds of errors is one of the characteristics that make us different from computers. Sometimes when we make these errors, the effects are relatively benign- we just get an error message and retype the entry. At other times, however, the software takes some action we did not expect. Your interface design should keep the user from making a disastrous error that is caused by a typo or a misspelling. Following the guidelines on the creation of commands (5-17 through 5-20) will help here, but, in addition, your software should check for obvious mistakes. It takes a good deal of experience working with a program to find these situations. They will show up, however, during testing. When they occur, the software should issue a prompt to ask the user to confirm what the software thinks the user was typing. For example:

```
You typed DE.  Do you mean DELETE (Y or N)?_
```

I do not mean to imply here that you issue this kind of prompt for every misspelling or typo, but only for those which have important consequences.

Figure 8-3   Error messages are always a surprise

Be as specific as possible in describing the cause of an error. Do not use error codes.(8-12)

Most of the error messages in Table 8-2 suffer from the problem that they do not tell the user what went wrong. This is the most common problem with error messages. Since it is not clear what caused the error, the user cannot use the information in the message to recover. Users, therefore, are likely to feel they cannot control the program.

Table 8-3 contains examples of some poor error messages which have been rewritten to improve them. The first example shows an error message that is vague and contains a meaningless error code. Notice how the rewritten message is specific in telling the user what went wrong.

TABLE 8-3   Examples of Poor and Improved Error Messages

Poor Error Message	Improved Error Message
1. ERROR 56 OPENING FILE.	The filename you typed cannot be found. Press F2 to list valid names.
2. JOB ABORTED! FILENAME ILLEGAL.	Retype filename. For example, REPORT.DOC
3. WRONG CHOICE.	Type an option from the menu.
4. YOU IDIOT, YOU MADE A STUPID MISTAKE ON CARD # 2. YOU PUNCHED 211 INSTEAD OF 112.	Card # 2 contains a 211 when 112 was expected.
5. THE LOCK MANAGER CANNOT PROCESS YOUR REQUEST NOW. PLEASE RETYPE YOUR REQUEST AFTER 6 pm.	Print requests of more than 50 pages cannot be run before 6 pm. Reenter your request at that time.
6. RETYPE THE NODE NAME AS SPECIFIED IN THE NETWORK MAP.	Retype the node name as either SI01 or SI02.
7. LOCKED FILE.	The file you requested, RE-PORT.DOC, is locked. Before you request the file again, type the following command: UNLOCK REPORT.DOC

Example 4 in the table shows the full text of the error message I discussed at the beginning of this chapter. This message has several problems with it, but it does have one good feature: it is specific. It tells the user exactly where the error occurred, what is wrong, and how to fix it. You may be insulted by the message, but at least you know how to avoid getting it again.

Example 1 in Table 8-3, in addition to being vague, also contains an error code. Error codes make users feel they are dealing directly with the inner workings of the computer. This violates one of the general principles, namely, that a good interface should shield the user from having to interact with the software that is doing the computing work. Occasionally, error codes are needed for some off-line analysis that may help you or an analyst improve a program. If this is the case, write the codes to a file which can later be examined rather than exposing the user to them.

Don't assign blame to the user or the software in an error message. Use a neutral tone.(8-13)

Consider these two error messages from Table 8-3:

1. WRONG CHOICE.
2. YOU IDIOT, YOU MADE A STUPID MISTAKE ON CARD # 2. YOU PUNCHED 211 INSTEAD OF 112.

Both error messages assign blame, to some degree, to the user. The first assigns blame subtly, while the second does it directly. There is a fine line between addressing the user directly and assigning blame. If you begin an error message with the word "you," it becomes very difficult to avoid blaming the user for causing the error. The examples in Table 8-4 show how to write messages that are more neutral in tone and do not blame the user for the error.

Whenever possible the error message should indicate what corrective action the user should take.(8-14)

None of the examples of poor messages in Table 8-3 tell the user how to correct the error. In many cases, knowing what went wrong is not enough. The user needs to know how to do it right. Most of the examples of improved messages in Table 8-3 provide some indication to the user about what action to take.   Often, explaining what to do will require a message that takes several lines. If there is no room on the screen for this detail, allow the user to display a separate help screen containing the more lengthy message. (See the next guideline.)

Consider describing error messages at more than one level of detail.(8-15)

If your error messages are specific and also tell users what corrective action to take, they can become lengthy. Sometimes this can be a disadvantage, especially when a frequently occurring message is displayed to experienced users who already know how to correct the problem. One way to get around this disadvantage is to provide two levels of detail for the message. The short version is displayed when the error occurs and users are then allowed to request the longer explanation by pressing a function key or issuing the command which requests help. Example 1 in Table 8-3 shows this format.

Be consistent in the format, wording, and placement of messages.(8-16)

Error messages, prompts, and status messages should be displayed either where users are working on the screen or at a location set aside for messages. Use similar formats for similar messages and, as with the other guidelines on consistency of wording, give words one and only one meaning and do not use two words to mean the same thing.

HELP!

As I stated earlier in this chapter, online help is a relatively new feature of software. Furthermore, the skills required to do it well are quite different from the skills needed to create the other components of the interface. Software designers who are trained in computer science are likely to be effective at designing a data entry display or a menu. Clearly explaining procedures or concepts in words, especially to new users, however, is as difficult for them as it is for anyone who is not a trained writer. Given the training and experience most designers have, it is not surprising online help is often less effective than it could be. Consider the example shown in Exhibit 8-3. This screen is intended to provide help on the Print command. Notice how it describes the internal workings of the printing process rather than the user's task. In addition, it does not address the user at all. It has an abstact, impersonal style that is typical of much data processing text.

These examples of poorly designed help suffer not only from wording that users cannot understand, but also from the way the information they contain is laid out. Keep in mind that from the user's point of view, help is never an end in itself, but is a means of finding out how to get some task done. Help text is a diversion that users request when they don't know what else to do. Often they are looking for one piece of information, a procedure, or a format, and they want to find it as quickly as possible and get back to work. Consequently, the layout and format of your help text should facilitate scanning as well as being understandable. The objective of this section is to describe the guidelines needed to create more effective help text.

Exhibit 8-3   An Example of Poor Help Text

```
PRINT

PRINT QUEUES A PRINT JOB TO A DESIGNATED SPOOLED DEVICE.
QUEUES MAY BE LOGICAL, PHYSICAL, BATCH OR GENERIC.  IF THE
INPUT FILES TO THE JOB DO NOT EXIST, THE JOB ABENDS.  THE JOB
ASSUMES DEFAULT NODES, DEVICES, AND DIRECTORIES UNLESS
OTHERWISE SPECIFIED.  IF SYS$PRINT IS ASSIGNED TO A SYSTEM
LP:, IT MUST BE REASSIGNED.  HIT <cr> TO INVOKE THE COMMAND
LEVEL.

SUBTOPIC?
```

Plan, draft, and evaluate your online help text.(8-17)

Following these steps will help you to create better online documentation. For further information about the writing process, see Redish (1983) and Felker and others (1981). These authors recommend the following steps in creating documentation:

1. Plan
       Think about the
             scope
             purpose
             audience
             reader's task
             constraints
2. Draft
       Work on the
             content
             organization
             language
             graphics
3. Evaluate
       Be sure to
             review
             revise
             edit
             test

Exhibit 8-4   Example of Help Text

Help on the COPY command.   Screen 1 of 4

The COPY command allows you to copy files and to combine files.

First, let's see how to copy files.

Copying a file from one disk to another. If you wish to copy a file called REPORT.DOC to another disk, follow these steps:

   1. Put the disk with the file on it into Drive A.

   2. Put the disk you want to copy the file to into Drive B.

   3. Type the following:

              COPY REPORT.DOC B:

This command will copy REPORT.DOC to the disk in Drive B. Be sure to put a space between the filename and the "B:". You could also use an equal sign. For example:

              COPY REPORT.DOC=B:

   Press F2 for more Help   Press RETURN to leave Help

The steps are grouped into three categories: plan, draft, and evaluate. Let's look at each of these three categories in detail. Throughout this discussion, I will be using the help text shown in Exhibit 8-4 as an example.

- Plan—Successful writers plan before they write, plan as they write, and plan again when they look at what they have written. Time spent planning will save time later. During your planning, you should answer these five questions:

   1. What is the scope of your help text? What's it about? Is it help on a word, a command, a procedure, a concept? The example shown in Exhibit 8-4 is help on how to use a command.

   2. What purpose will the help serve? This is an important question for you to answer about your help text because it will allow you to more clearly define your goals. Many times the purpose of help is only to remind the user about some procedure or concept which is explained more fully in a tutorial or in a paper document. If this if your goal, your purpose is to remind, not to instruct. Frequently, however, help is used to substitute for a tutorial. Its purpose is to explain to an inexperienced user how to execute a command

or procedure. If this is your goal, your purpose is to instruct the user and you will have to provide a great deal more detail. The "Copy" example in Exhibit 8-4 is closer to being a tutorial-like help than a reminder-type help.

3. Who is the audience? Is it new users or experienced users or both? Are they engineers or managers? The words you choose and the level of detail required will depend on your audience. The example in Exhibit 8-4 is intended for new users.

4. What tasks will the reader be performing? Is the reader looking for information to understand the choices on a menu or how to perform a complex series of steps in which the format of the entered data must be exact? In the example in Exhibit 8-4, the reader is looking for the procedure needed to copy a file. The important information is the list of steps to complete this procedure.

5. What constraints limit you? In the case of online help, the constraints are severe. Most computer terminal screens will allow you to display only about twenty lines of text. The contrast available on most screens also makes it much more difficult to read text on a screen than on paper. In addition, users do not like to read long text paragraphs on a screen. You will find that you are limited to putting only a few lines of text on a screen. The "Copy" example in Exhibit 8-4 fills an entire screen but contains only a small amount of information. Several of the guidelines in this section describe ways to deal with these constraints.

• Draft—When your planning is complete and you are ready to begin to write your help text, follow these steps:

1. Identify the content of the help text. Given your answers to the five planning questions, what is it you want to say?

2. Organize your text. Organization is always a critical part of writing, but it is especially important for online help. The constraints imposed by the medium make it critical to carefully consider the order with which you express your content and the ways you can convey it by using lists, tables, and examples instead of plain text. (See Guideline 8-21 below.)

3. Write your help in plain English. This is the same concept I have been stressing throughout this book. Don't use computer jargon, and do express your ideas in short, complete sentences.

4. Use graphics whenever you can. Pictures are indeed worth a thousand words. Use diagrams, maps, etc. to explain concepts.

- Evaluate—After the draft is done you will have to review, revise, and edit it. To do this effectively, you must have other people read it. You can begin with your colleagues, but you must not stop there. Otherwise you will end up with text which only computer-literate people can understand. You need to have potential users read and attempt to use your help text. The best way to do this is to include the help text in the usability tests of the software and the paper documentation. This means exposing potential users to the software and having them try to achieve a clearly stated objective with it. (See Chapter 2.) After the test, revise your text and test it again until it meets your objectives.

Write in short, complete sentences; punctuate each sentence.(8-18)

Help text should be simply stated, but not telegraphic. Use complete sentences with appropriate punctuation and make them short. As a rule of thumb, sentences of less than twenty words are recommended.

Write sentences in the positive or simple negative. Avoid the passive voice and do not use double negatives.(8-19)

If you address the user directly, it will be natural to express your sentences in the positive and simple negative. Research has shown that it is easier for people to comprehend these sentence types (Gough 1965). The passive voice is often awkward and therefore more difficult to understand. You will be tempted to use a passive voice when you are trying to explain some action of the software such as "A message is displayed by the system" or "The filename will be assigned by the text editor." Turn these sentences around to the active voice: "The system will display a message" or "The text editor will assign the filename." Finally, never use a double negative. It not only is gramatically poor, it also will confuse the user.

Write short paragraphs.(8-20)

A large block of text looks much more formidable on a screen than it does on paper. In addition, in my experience, people do not like to sit at the screen and read lengthy descriptions. Remember that reading text on a screen takes almost one-fourth longer than it does on paper. Try to make your paragraphs of help text no more than three or four lines long even if a paragraph consists of only one sentence. You can minimize the amount of running text you need by using the following guideline.

Use bullets, numbered lists, and tables to make it easier to find the most important information. Leave ample open space.(8-21)

The example help screen shown in Exhibit 8-4 is relatively easy to follow. Its format allows users to quickly scan it to find what they need. Contrast that format with the following paragraph which expresses the same content with running text:

The COPY command allows you to copy files and to combine files. First, let's see how to copy a file. If you wish to copy a file called REPORT.DOC from one disk to another, you would first put the disk with the file on it into Drive A, then put the disk that you want to copy the file to into Drive B, then type the command COPY REPORT.DOC B:. This command will copy REPORT.DOC to the disk in Drive B. Be sure to put a space between the file name and the "B:". You could also use an equal sign in the command. For example, COPY REPORT.DOC=B:.

What is wrong with this paragraph? Not its wording, but its layout. It does not lead the reader's eye to the important information.

To improve the layout of your help text, break it up with bullets, lists, and tables.

- Use bulleted lists when you have options to explain. Whenever you have a sentence that lists options with commas between them, consider breaking up the text into a bulleted list.
- Use numbered lists to show the steps in a process.

- Use a table when you have two or more categories of
  information to explain, such as

Choose this option	If you want to do this
C	Create a new document
E	Edit an existing document
A	Attach one document to another
S	Send a document

Use examples to show users what they should type and what the results will look
like.(8-22)

One of the most frustrating features of traditional help
messages is that they do not show you what a command or data
entry will look like when you type it. Many people find learning by
example much easier than learning by explanation. In addition,
examples are especially helpful when the purpose of help is to
remind the user about the details of a procedure or format. Notice
that none of the examples of poor help messages shown in Exhibits
8-1, 8-2, and 8-3 contain an example. Contrast this with Exhibit 8-
4, which leads your eye immediately to the examples that show you
what a "COPY" command looks like.

Do not expect the user to read more than about three screens of help at one
time.(8-23)

In addition to the impatience users often show with reading
running text, they also can become impatient with a help message
that carries over to multiple screens. Remember, the user is in the
process of trying to accomplish some task and the help is a diversion
from that process. About three screens of help is the normal limit I
have observed. Unfortunately, the amount of information that can
be displayed on a screen is quite small. It does not take much information to fill three screens. This constraint can be a serious one
if the purpose of your help is to instruct rather than to be a memory
aid.

One solution to this constraint is to have a separate tutorial for
your application and to refer the user to the appropriate tutorial
section in the help text. Tutorials can be expensive to create, but
they often more than pay for themselves over the lifecycle of an

application. The other solution is just to try harder to break up the help into smaller packets.

Use online help to explain concepts, procedures, messages, menu choices, commands, words, function keys, and formats.(8-24)

During the planning stage of document design you will have to define the scope of the help that you will provide online. Your first and most difficult problem will be deciding how to limit what you provide help on. Table 8-4 contains a list of most of the categories of online help that I have seen and some specific examples of each. You will have to decide which categories your users will need. You cannot write help text for every word and every procedure in the software. How can you decide where help is needed? There are three sources of information that can help you:

- Online help from other programs. Every time you use a program that contains help, look at the help, analyze it, make notes about it, and file your notes. Whenever you are trying to decide what to write help on, go back to your notes to look for examples that may be relevant to your application.
- Your own experience with the software. There is no substitute for using the software yourself. You must gain access to it as it is being developed and work with it. As you exercise it, view your experience from the perspective of a potential user. Chances are very good that whenever you have a problem, the user will also. These problem areas are some of the places where help will be needed.
- The results of testing. Creating effective help text is one of the many areas that benefit from usability testing. You will, of course, need to test the help text you create. During testing you will also find new areas where help is needed. As you observe people using the software, look for situations where they are confused and/or making errors. One solution to improving the usability of the software is to provide some form of online help for these situations. You may even find that help is the only way to get users past a design error which can't be fixed until the next release of the product.

From these three sources you should be able to identify the areas that will require help text.

TABLE 8-4   Categories and Examples of Online Help

- Help on Help
    - How do I get help?
- Help on Concepts
    - How is the program structured?
    - What is a spreadsheet?
- Help on System Procedures
    - How do I save a file?
    - How do I format a diskette?
- Help on Application Procedures
    - How do I cut and paste text?
    - How do I find an item in the data base?
- Help on Messages
    - Error- What are the valid file names?
    - Status- What does "90% FREE" mean?
- Help on Menu choices
    - What does "Defer a message" mean?
    - What does "Export a message" mean?
- Help on Function Keys
    - What do the keys on the numeric key pad do?
    - What does BREAK do?
- Help on Commands
    - How do I use COPY?
    - How do I use SHIP?
- Help on Words
    - What does "Import" mean?
    - What does "Merge" mean?
- Help on Formats
    - How do I enter times in twenty-four hour format?
    - How do I indicate margins in inches rather than pitch?

Provide users with an orientation to the structure of the software.(8-25)

Of all the categories of help shown in Table 8-4, help on concepts deserves special attention. There are several cognitive theorists who believe that when new users operate a program, they attempt to build a mental model or picture of the structure of the program (Norman 1983; Saja 1985).   In effect, they are trying to discover the structure the designer has put into the program- not the physical structure, but the conceptual structure.   There are several recent empirical studies that verify this theoretical concept. They show that users are more productive and make fewer errors with programs that are new to them when they are shown a pictorial "map" of the structure of the program before they use it (Billingsley 1982; Parton and others 1984).   This type of high-level information is critical to new users.   Part of the reason early spreadsheet programs were so successful, despite their poor interfaces, was that the people who used them understood the concept of a spreadsheet.   It was obvious to them how a spreadsheet worked, since they used paper versions frequently.   The structure of most applications is not so obvious, however.

Users must build their mental model of the structure of the program from the interface they use.   When the interface is confusing, the user's mental model will be poorly structured.   As a result, the user will have trouble predicting how the program will react to transactions.

If you follow the guidelines in this book, the user will be better able to form a mental model of the program which is precise and accurate.   In addition, you can directly influence this process by providing the user with graphics and high-level concepts which explain the structure of the program.   For example, if your program contains a four-level hierarchy of menus, show the users this hierarchy and indicate how they can tell where they are in the structure and how they can move through it.   Put this information in an option such as "New User Help" and make it available on the main menu or from the first screen users see.

Whenever possible display help text on the screen with the application.(8-26)

One of the potential advantages of online documentation is that it is available when the user needs it.   When users want help, they do not have to go to a manual to find it, they can call it up on the screen.   This advantage, however, is partially negated when the user has to call up help on a separate screen from the application, read it, and then return to the application to complete a procedure. This is especially true when the help describes a multi-step procedure or a complex format.   In fact, a recent study suggests that, at least for a text editing task, users perform better when help is in paper form rather than on a separate help screen (Cohill and Williges 1985). In that study, it was more helpful to be able to read the help text on paper and compare it to the application than it was to read a separate help screen and go back to the application.

To avoid this problem, display the help on the application screen whenever you can. If your help system is extensive, it is worth using a scrolled area on the top or bottom of the screen or assigning a separate window into which help can be displayed. If the software or your budget do not allow you to do this, keep this limitation in mind when you are drafting your help text. Put in special reminders to users at the end of the help so that they can remember the critical information as they go back to the application.

Use context-sensitive help only if you are sure what the user needs help with. (8-27)

The term "context-sensitive help" is one of the buzz words of the user-interface literature. It refers to the ability of software to respond to users' requests for help with the information they need without requiring users to be very specific. The user simply asks for help in the context of performing a task and the software "knows" what help the user needs. For example, if users are editing a document and have selected a paragraph to work on but do not remember the command or function key to move the text to another part of the document, they can request help and the software will explain how to move text.

In principle, context-sensitive help is a great concept. Frequently, however, it is ineffective. It is not always possible for you to anticipate what help the user wants. In the above example, how do you know whether the user wants to move the paragraph or copy it or delete it? The only way to handle this situation is to provide users with a list of the possible actions they can do on a paragraph and allow them to pick what they need. This is context-sensitive help, but in a weaker sense.

If you can be sure what the user wants help on, then make a specific, context-sensitive help message available at that point. A data entry field is one case where it is usually clear what help to provide. However, if there is any doubt about the help the user needs, provide a more general help message with instructions for branching to more specific messages.

Provide a direct route back to the application task.(8-28)

Users should be able to leave every help screen by pressing a single key and be returned to the screen from which they requested help. It should always be clear to the user which key performs this function. This is sometimes achieved by displaying a status message at the bottom of each screen, such as "Press RETURN to exit help" or "Press RETURN to go back to the screen where you were working."

Be consistent in the format and wording of help text.(8-29)

To assist the user in recognizing the various types of help being provided, format them consistently. For example, whenever you are describing a procedure, set it off in paragraphs that begin

```
Step 1
Step 2
. . .
Step N
```

Whenever you give an example of what the user should type, display it in capitals, such as

```
COPY REPORT.DOC
```

If you format your help consistently, it will be more effective.

Follow the guidelines for displaying text in your help messages.(8-30)

In Chapter 6 there is a set of guidelines which apply to all text displays. These guidelines should, of course, be followed when you create your help text. In particular, you should

- Put a title on every screen.(6-1)
- Use lower case characters in running text.(6-8)
- Left justify text but leave a ragged right margin.(6-9)
- Put at least one blank line between paragraphs.(6-8)
- Avoid hyphenation(6-10)
- Avoid unfamiliar abbreviations.(6-11)

Appendix

A List of the Guidelines

This appendix contains a list of the guidelines that are described in Chapters 5 through 8. They are repeated here to make it convenient for you to scan them.

CONTROLLING TRANSACTIONS

- Choose the transaction control method that is appropriate for the anticipated level of computer experience of users and for the performance objectives of the application.(5-1) (Page 61)
- Put a meaningful title on the top of every menu.(5-2) (Page 68)
- For full-screen menus, provide symmetric balance by centering the title and the menu options around the center axis of the screen.(5-3) (Page 68)
- Choose an organizing principle for the menu options.(5-4) (Page 69)
- To facilitate scanning, put blank lines between logical groupings of menu options and after about every fifth option in a long list.(5-5) (Page 70)
- Limit the number of menu choices to one screen.(5-6) (Page 70)
- Use an option selection method that is consistent with the technology available at the user's work station and the size of the application being designed.(5-7) (Page 71)
- Provide a way for the user to leave the menu without choosing an option.(5-8) (Page 72)
- Use words for your menu options that clearly and specifically describe what the user is selecting; use simple, active verbs to describe menu options.(5-9) (Page 73)
- Use icons that unambiguously identify the meaning of the user's options.(5-10) (Page 75)
- Minimize the highlighting used on a menu.(5-11) (Page 76)
- Do not require the user to enter leading or trailing blanks or zeros, and do not include a default value on a menu.(5-12) (Page 76)
- Display the menu options in mixed, upper and lower case letters. (5-13) (Page 77)
- Organize menu hierarchies according to the tasks users will perform, rather than the structure of the software modules.(5-14) (Page 77)
- Use function keys sparingly to speed up the execution of frequently used operations.(5-15) (Page 79)

- Be sure that any function keys that you use will operate correctly on all of the keyboards users have.(5-16) (Page 80)
- Use common, short English words that clearly describe the action that the command will carry out; choose words that are distinctive from one another.(5-17) (Page 81)
- Allow the user to shorten commands by using a consistent rule for abbreviating them.(5-18) (Page 82)
- Allow the user to stack a series of commands on one line.(5-19) (Page 83)
- Allow the user to display a list of commands.(5-20) (Page 83)
- Be consistent in the use of menu formats, procedures, and wording; the mapping of keys to functions; the naming and abbreviation of commands; and the design of question-and-answer prompts.(5-21) (Page 84)

DISPLAYING INFORMATION

- Put a title on every display screen that clearly and specifically describes the contents of the screen.(6-1) (Page 88)
- Display only information that the user needs to know.(6-2) (Page 88)
- Display data to the user in directly usable form.(6-3) (Page 89)
- Provide symmetric balance to displays by centering titles and headings and by placing information on both sides of the center axis.(6-4) (Page 89)
- Every display should indicate how to exit from the screen.(6-5) (Page 90)
- When displays continue over multiple screens, the screen should indicate where the user is in the display.(6-6) (Page 90)
- Consider the skills of your users and the information they will manipulate when you display information in multiple windows.(6-7) (Page 91))
- Display text conventionally in mixed, upper and lower case and with appropriate punctuation. Put a blank line between each paragraph and double-space text whenever you can.(6-8) (Page 92)
- Left justify text but leave a ragged right margin.(6-9) (Page 93)
- Avoid hyphenation of words between lines.(6-10) (Page 94)

- Use abbreviations and acronyms only when they are significantly shorter than the full text *and* when they will be understood by the user.(6-11) (Page 94)
- Put a meaningful label, in upper case letters on the columns and, if appropriate, the rows of tables and lists. Continue the labels when a table or list extends over more than one screen.(6-12) (Page 95)
- Arrange the items in a table or list in some recognizable order to facilitate scanning.(6-13) (Page 96)
- Put items in a multiple column list in vertical columns which are read from left to right on the screen.(6-14) (Page 96)
- Left justify columns of alphabetic data; right justify columns of numeric data or align them by the decimal point or other delimiter.(6-15) (Page 96)
- Insert a blank line after about every fifth row in a long column.(6-16) (Page 97)
- Put at least two spaces between the longest item in a column and the beginning of the next column.(6-17) (Page 98)
- Start with a "1" not a "0" when listed items are labeled by number.(6-18) (Page 98)
- Break up long strings of alphanumeric characters into smaller groups of three to four characters each.(6-19) (Page 98)
- Use highlighting to emphasize important information only. Do not overuse it.(6-20) (Page 99)
- Use blinking and audible tones to highlight only critical information that requires an immediate response from the user. Turn them off as soon as the user has made that response.(6-21) (Page 100)
- Select a highlighting method that is appropriate for the level of importance of the information being emphasized and for the layout of the screen on which it will be displayed.(6-22) (Page 101)
- When the user must read the information that is being highlighted, do not use a highlighting method which reduces the legibility of the information being emphasized.(6-23) (Page 102)
- Select colors from the center of the color spectrum. Select color combinations that complement each other.(6-24) (Page 103)
- Be consistent in the layout of displays and in the way that you highlight information.(6-25) (Page 104)

ENTERING DATA

- When the user must transcribe data directly from a paper form to the screen, the layout of the screen should be similar to the layout of the paper form.(7-1) (Page 108)
- Group data fields into logical categories on the screen; provide a header that describes the contents of each category.(7-2) (Page 108)
- Make areas of the screen not needed for data entry or commands inaccessible to the user.(7-3) (Page 109)
- Never require the user to enter information which is already available to the software or can be computed by it.(7-4) (Page 110)
- Do not require the user to enter dimensional units.(7-5) (Page 111)
- Allow the user to enter data by character replacement.(7-6) (Page 111)
- Put a caption describing the data to be entered adjacent to each data field; incorporate memory joggers into the caption.(7-7) (Page 112)
- Justify data entries automatically.(7-8) (Page 113)
- Display default values in data fields when appropriate.(7-9) (Page 113)
- Provide context-sensitive help for data entry fields.(7-10) (Page 113)
- Allow the user to move freely through the fields in a data entry screen.(7-11) (Page 114)
- Allow the user to work on the whole data entry screen before transmitting the data to the application program.(7-12) (Page 115)
- Allow the user to leave the data entry screen without filling in any data.(7-13) (Page 115)
- Each key used in a data entry screen should have one and only one function.(7-14) (Page 116)
- Provide users with either a status message on the data entry screen or a help message that shows the mapping of keys to functions.(7-15) (Page 117)
- Be consistent in the design of data entry screens, fields, and procedures.(7-16) (Page 117)

SMOOTHING COMMUNICATION WITH ONLINE DOCUMENTATION

- Write online documentation in plain English.(8-1) (Page 125)
- Address the user directly as "you;" use the active voice.(8-2) (Page 125)
- Use simple action verbs to describe procedures. Don't use nouns to replace pronouns, verbs, and adjectives.(8-3) (Page 127)
- Describe procedures in logical order.(8-4) (Page 127)
- Use simple English words, not computer or other jargon.(8-5) (Page 127)
- Avoid humor in online documentation.(8-6) (Page 130)
- Use status messages to tell the user what the software is doing, where the user is in a sequence, and what options the user has selected or are available.(8-7) (Page 134)
- Use prompts to ask the user to make a simple choice or to enter data or commands. Be as specific as possible.(8-8) (Page 137)
- Include memory aids in the prompt to make formats, infrequently-used processes, or exceptions to normal practice clear.(8-9) (Page 138)
- When defaults are allowed with prompts, indicate clearly which default value will be initiated.(8-10) (Page 138)
- Design your software to check for obvious errors.(8-11) (Page 139)
- Be as specific as possible in describing the cause of an error. Do not use error codes.(8-12) (Page 141)
- Don't assign blame to the user or the software in an error message. Use a neutral tone.(8-13) (Page 143)
- Whenever possible the error message should indicate what corrective action the user should take.(8-14) (Page 143)
- Consider describing error messages at more than one level of detail.(8-15) (Page 143)
- Be consistent in the format, wording, and placement of messages.(8-16) (Page 144)
- Plan, draft, and evaluate your online help text.(8-17) (Page 145)
- Write in short, complete sentences; punctuate each sentence.(8-18) (Page 148)

- Write sentences in the positive or simple negative. Avoid the passive voice and do not use double negatives.(8-19) (Page 148)
- Write short paragraphs.(8-20) (Page 149)
- Use bullets, numbered lists, and tables to make it easier to find the most important information. Leave ample open space.(8-21) (Page 149)
- Use examples to show users what they should type and what the results will look like.(8-22) (Page 150)
- Do not expect the user to read more than about three screens of help at one time.(8-23) (Page 150)
- Use online help to explain concepts, procedures, messages, menu choices, commands, words, function keys, and formats.(8-24) (Page 151)
- Provide users with an orientation to the structure of the software.(8-25) (Page 152)
- Whenever possible display help text on the screen with the application.(8-26) (Page 153)
- Use context-sensitive help only if you are sure what the user needs help with.(8-27) (Page 154)
- Provide a direct route back to the application task.(8-28) (Page 155)
- Be consistent in the format and wording of help text.(8-29) (Page 155)
- Follow the guidelines for displaying text in your help messages.(8-30) (Page 155)

References

Ausubel, D., In defense of advanced organizers: A reply to the critics, *Review of Educational Research*, 1978, 48, 251-257.

Baroudi, J., Olson, M., and Ives, B., An empirical study of the impact of user involvement on system usage and information satisfaction, *Communications of the ACM*, 1986, 29, 232-238.

Billingsley, Patricia, Navigation through hierarchical menu structures: Does it help to have a map? *Proceedings of the Human Factors Society- 26th Annual Meeting*, 1982, 103-107.

Bly, S. A. and Rosenberg, J. K., A comparison of tiled and overlapping windows, *Proceedings of CHI'86 Human Factors in Computing Systems, Boston, April 13-17, 1986*, ACM, New York, 101-106.

Brown, C. M., Burkleo, H., Mangledorf, J., Olsen, R. and Williams, A., *Human Factors Engineering Standards for Information Processing Systems*, Sunnyvale, CA:Lockheed Missiles and Space Co. Inc., 1981.

Chase, P., *The power of words*, New York: Harcourt Brace Janovich, 1953.

Cohen, E., Smith, E., and Iverson, L., Constraint-based tiled windows, *IEEE Computer Graphics and Applications*, 1986, 6, 35-45.

Cohill, A. and Willigies, R., Retrieval of HELP information for novice users of interactive computer systems, *Human Factors*, 1985, 27, 335-343.

Dooling, D. and Mullet, P., Locus of thematic effects in retention of prose, *Journal of Experimental Psychology*, 1973, 97, 404-406.

Dumas, J., The role of human factors in software development, *Proceedings of National Computer Graphics Association*. Anaheim, CA, May, 1986, Volume III, 530-539.

Dumas, J., and Redish, J., Using plain English in designing the user interface, *Proceedings of the Human Factors Society 30th Annual Meeting*, Dayton, OH, October, 1986, Volume II, 1207-1211.

Engel,Stephen,and Granda,Richard, *Guidelines for Man / Display Interfaces*, IBM Technical Report No., TR00.2720, 1975.

Ehrenreich, S. and Porcu, T., Abbreviations for automated systems: Teaching operators the rules, In A. Badre and B. Shneiderman, *Directions in Human Computer Interaction*, New Jersey:Ablex Publishing Co., 1982.

Ehrenreich, S., Computer abbreviations: Evidence and synthesis, *Human Factors*, 1985, 27, 143-155.

Felker, G. and others, *Guidelines for Document Designers*, Washington, D.C.: American Institutes for Research, 1981.

Galitz, W., *Handbook of Screen Format Design*, Wellesley, MA: QED Information Sciences, 1981.

Gould, J. and others, Why is reading slower from CRT displays than from paper, *Proceedings of the Human Factors Society 30th Annual Meeting*, Dayton, OH, October, 1986, Volume I, 834-835.

Gough, P., Grammatical transformations and speed of understanding, *Journal of Verbal Learning and Verbal Behavior*, 1965, 4, 107-111.

Higgins, D., *Data Structured Software Maintenance*, New York: Dorset House Publishing Co., 1986.

Kiger, John, The depth/breadth trade-off in the design of menu-driven user interfaces, *International Journal of Man-Machine Studies*, 1984, 20, 201-213.

King, D., *Current practices in software development*, New York: Yourdon Press, Inc., 1984.

Kruk, R. and Muter, P., Reading of continuous text on video screens, *Human Factors*, 1984, 26, 339-345.

Lodding, K., Iconic interfacing, *IEEE Computer Graphics and Applications*, 1983, 3, 11-24.

MacGregor, J. and Newman, L., Optimizing the structure of database menu indexes: A decision model of menu search, *Human Factors*, 1986, 28, 387-399.

Magers, C., An experimental evaluation of online HELP for non-programmers, *Proceedings of Chi'83 Human Factors in Computing Systems*, Boston, December 12-15, 1983, ACM, New York, 277-281.

Martin, J. and McClure, C., *Diagramming Techniques for Analysts and Programmers*, New Jersey: Prentice-Hall, 1985.

McNulty, J. A., An analysis of recall and recognition processes in verbal learning, *Journal of Verbal Learning and Verbal Behavior*, 1965, 4, 430-435.

Mills, C.B. and Weldon, L.J., Reading from computer screens, Tech. Report No. CAR-TR-94, Human-Computer Interaction Laboratory, Center for Automation Research, Univ. of Maryland, October, 1984.

Murch, G. M., Physiological principles for the effective use of color, *IEEE Computer Graphics and Applications*, November, 1984, 49-55.

Muter, P., Latremouille, S., Treurniet, W. and Beam, P., Extended reading of continuous text on television screens, *Human Screens*, 1982, 24, 501-508.

Myers, B., The importance of percent-done progress indicators for computer-human interfaces, *Proceedings of CHI'85 Human Factors in Computing Systems*, San Francisco, April 14-18, 1985, ACM, New York, 11-17.

Newell, A., The prospects of science in human-computer interaction, *Human-Computer Interaction*, 1986. (In press.)

Nickerson, R., On conversatinal interactions with computers, in S. Trew (Ed.), *User-Oriented Design of Interactive Graphic Systems*, Proceedings of the ACM/SIGRAPH, Pittsburgh, PA, October 1976.

Norman, Donald, Design principles for human-computer interfaces, *Proceedings of CHI'83 Human Factors in Computing Systems*, Boston, December 1983, New York: ACM, pp 1-10.

Paap, K. and Roske-Hoftstrand, R. The optimum number of menu options per panel, *Human Factors*, 1986, 28, 377-385.

Pace, B., Color combinations and contrast reversals on visual display units, *Proceedings of the Human Factors Society 26th Annual Meeting*, San Antonio, 1984, pp 326-330.

Parkinson, S., Sisson, N. and Snowberry, K., Organization of broad computer menu displays, *International Journal of Man-Machine Studies*, 1985, 23, 689-697.

Parton, D., Huffman, K., Pridgen, P., Norman, K. and Shneiderman, B., Learning a menu selection tree: Training methods compared, Report No. CAR-TR-66, University of Maryland: Center for Automation Research.

Pew, R. and Rollins, A., *Dialog Specification Procedures*, Report 3129, Cambridge, MA:Bolt, Beranek and Newman, 1975.

Redish, J., The Plain English Movement, in S. Greenbaum, Ed. *The English Language Today*, New York: Pergamon Press, 1985.

Redish, V., Using cognitive science in developing materials to train writers, *Technology of Training Evaluation and Productivity Assesement*, Society of Applied Learning Technology, 1983.

Saja, Allan, The cognitive model: An approach to designing the human-computer interface, *SIGCHI Bulletin*, 1985, 16, 36-40.

Schell, D. Usability testing of screen design: Beyond standards, principles and guidelines, *Proceedings of the Human Factors Society 30th Annual Meeting*, Dayton, OH, October, 1986, 1212-1215.

Shneiderman, B., System message design: Guidelines and experimental results, In A. Badre and B. Shneiderman, *Directions in Human Computer Interaction*, New Jersey: Ablex Publishing Co., 1982.

Smith, D., Designing the Star user interface, *BYTE*, April, 1982, 242-282.

Smith, P., Janosky, B. and Hildreth, C., Study of the errors committed in the use of an online library catalog system, *Proceedings of the Human Factors Society 28th Annual Meeting*, San Antonio, 1984, 639-642.

Smith, S. and Mosier, J., Design guidelines for user-system interface software, *Technical Report ESD-TR-84-190*, 1984, Hanscom AFB, MA: USAF Electronic Systems Division.

Smith, S. and Mosier, J., *Guidelines for designing user interface software*, Technical Report ESD-TR-86-278, 1986, Hanscom AFB, MA: USAF Electronic Systems Division.

Snowberry, Kathleen, Parkinson, Stanley, and Sisson, Norwood, Computer display menus, *Ergonomics*, 1983, 26,699-712.

Taylor, J. M. and Murch, G.M., The effective use of color in computer graphics application, *Proceedings of the National Computer Graphics Association Annual Conference*, Anahiem, CA., 1986,Vol. III, 515-521.

Tinker, M., *Legibility of Print*, Ames,IA: Iowa State University Press, 1969.

Trollip, S. and Sales, G., Readability of computer-generated fill-justified text, *Human Factors*, 1986, 28, 159-164.

Turing, A. Computing machinery and intelligence, *Mind*, 1950, 59, 433-460.

Vartabedian, A.G., The effects of letter size, case and generation method on CRT display search time, *Human Factors*, 1971, 13, 363-368.

Yourdon, E. and Constantine, L., *Structured Design*, Englewood Cliffs, New Jersey: Prentice-Hall, 1979.

Zolton, E., How acceptable are computers to professional persons, *Proceedings of Human Factors in Computer Systems*, Gaithersburg, MD, 1982, 74-77.

Index

A

Abbreviations, 81, 82, 84, 86, 94, 131, 155
  truncation of, 82, 83
Audible tone, 86, 99, 100–102
Ausubel, D., 88, 166

B

Baroudi, J., 24, 166
Billingsley, P., 153, 166
Blinking, 57, 76, 86, 99–102
Bly, S. A., 91, 166
Brown, C. M., 71, 166

C

Captions, data entry, 56, 106, 109–14, 122
Case:
  lower, 77, 86, 92, 131, 138, 155
  upper, 77, 86, 92, 131, 138
Chase, P., 125, 166
Cohen, E., 92, 166
Cohill, A., 54, 154, 166
Color, 76, 86, 99, 100–104
Command language, 7, 36, 81–83
Commands, 4, 60–65, 81–87, 130, 151–54
  stacking of, 83
Consistency, 2, 36–38, 45, 48, 50–53, 55, 84, 104, 117
Constantine, L., 21, 168
Creativity, 19, 40, 41
Cursor, 61, 71, 72, 86, 109, 110–12, 117

D

Data entry, 105–18
  captions, 56, 106, 109–15, 154
  fields, 106, 108, 109, 111–15, 154

procedures, 106–8, 114, 117
screens, 34, 87, 89, 106–10, 114–17, 138, 144
Default value, 76, 77, 111, 113, 138, 139
Dialogue, question-and-answer, 52, 60–62, 84
Display of:
  numbers, 57
  tables, 56, 86, 87, 95–97
  text, 57, 86, 89, 90, 93
  titles, 57
Documentation:
  online (*see* Online documentation)
  print (*see* Print documentation)
Dooling, D., 88, 166
Dumas, J., 23, 125, 166

E

Ehrenreich, S., 82, 166
Engel, S., 66, 166
English, plain, 54, 73, 120, 125, 127, 147

F

Felker, G., 145, 166
Fields, data entry (*see* Data entry, fields)
FORTRAN, 53
Function keys, 34, 39, 52, 60, 61, 63, 65, 72, 79, 80, 81, 84, 106, 117

G

Galitz, W., 108, 166
Glossary, 34, 40, 74–75, 81
Gough, P., 148, 166
Gould, J., 124, 166
Granada, R., 66, 166
Graphics, display of, 5, 48, 50, 56

Announcing. . . .

The Annual Prentice Hall Professional/Technical/Reference Catalog: Books For Computer Scientists, Computer/Electrical Engineers and Electronic Technicians

- Prentice Hall, the leading publisher of Professional/Technical/Reference books in the world, is pleased to make its vast selection of titles in computer science, computer/electrical engineering and electronic technology more accessible to all professionals in these fields through the publication of this new catalog!

- If your business or research depends on timely, state-of-the-art information, The Annual Prentice Hall Professional/Technical/Reference Catalog: Books For Computer Scientists, Computer/Electrical Engineers and Electronic Technicians was designed especially for you! Titles appearing in this catalog will be grouped according to interest areas. Each entry will include: title, author, author affiliations, title description, table of contents, title code, page count and copyright year.

- In addition, this catalog will also include advertisements of new products and services from other companies in key high tech areas.

SPECIAL OFFER!

- Order your copy of The Annual Prentice Hall Professional/Technical/Reference Catalog: Books For Computer Scientists, Computer/Electrical Engineers and Electronic Technicians for only $2.00 and receive $5.00 off the purchase of your first book from this catalog. In addition, this catalog entitles you to special discounts on Prentice Hall titles in computer science, computer/electrical engineering and electronic technology.

Please send me _____ copies of The Annual Prentice Hall Professional/Technical/Reference Catalog (title code: 62280–3)

SAVE!

If payment accompanies order, plus your state's sales tax where applicable, Prentice Hall pays postage and handling charges. Same return privilege refund guaranteed. Please do not mail cash.

- ☐ PAYMENT ENCLOSED—shipping and handling to be paid by publisher (please include your state's tax where applicable).
- ☐ BILL ME for The Annual Prentice Hall Professional/Technical/Reference Catalog (with small charge for shipping and handling).

Mail your order to: Prentice Hall, Book Distribution Center,
Route 59 at Brook Hill Drive,
West Nyack, N.Y. 10994

Name _____

Address _____

City _____ State _____ Zip _____

I prefer to charge my   ☐ Visa   ☐ MasterCard

Card Number _____ Expiration Date _____

Signature _____

Offer not valid outside the United States.

DESIGNING USER INTERFACES FOR SOFTWARE

JOSEPH S. DUMAS

By taking the user's point of view, author Joseph Dumas narrows the gap between technology and its application. The theme of his book is that computer software must designed from the user's viewpoint and tested with potential users to ensure that they readily make it work. Designers of software and its users communicate through the in face to the software; designers who already realize this have taken the first step towa creating better products. Help is found in the rules and guidelines described in this b

The components of the user-software interface that the book is primarily concerned with are: the words and symbols that people see and read on a computer screen; the content and layout of displays; the procedures that people must use to enter, store, ar display information; and the organizational structures of the interface as a whole. The goal is to help create better, more effective user interfaces. The audience for which th book is designed includes:

- professionals who create software,
- project managers who guide its development, and
- students who are learning about software development.

The material in the book comes from three major sources: the author's experience working with software designers to help create and evaluate products, his experience training as a cognitive psychologist, and recent research on human-computer interact After thousands of hours of working with software engineers and programmers, the au saw the need for a single source that describes and interprets the accumulated knowledge about human-computer interaction and tells users how their organization c improve the user interfaces to all their future products. This book is the answer to that need.

About the Author
JOSEPH S. DUMAS (Ph.D., State University of New York at Buffalo) has more than 15 years of experience working in human factors research and development. He has taug at Oakland University, where he conducted and published research on human decisio making. His courses there included studies of human learning and memory, and use computers in psychological research. At the U.S. Department of Transportation, Dr. Du conducted and published human factors research on the impact of computer-based systems on personnel. He developed and evaluated the man/machine interface to complex command and control systems. Presently, Dr. Dumas is the Senior Research Scientist in the Systems Division at the American Institutes for Research, where he provides consulting services to business and government in the planning, design, and evaluation of user interfaces to new computer-based products. With this experience, Dr. Dumas is uniquely qualified to write on the design of user interfaces for software.

PRENTICE HALL, Englewood Cliffs, NJ 07632

ISBN 0-13-201971